Konrad Onasch

RUSSIAN ICONS

PHAIDON

Translated by I. Grafe

Phaidon Press Limited, Littlegate House, St Ebbe's Street, Oxford
Published in the United States of America by E. P. Dutton, New York

First published in English 1977

Originally published in German under the title Altrussische Ikonen

ISBN 0 7148 1792 9
Library of Congress Catalog Card Number: 77-75399

Printed in the German Democratic Republic

RUSSIAN ICONS

Shortly before the end of the tenth century, the Grand-Prince Vladimir of Kiev was baptized and established Christianity of the Byzantine rite as the official religion of his people. The sumptuous, mysterious ritual of the Orthodox Church was introduced into Rus (Old Russia), and with it also the icons, those distinctive paintings which were rooted in Christian dogma and conformed strictly to Biblical and hagiographical prototypes, and are to that extent quite unlike the gentler and more spontaneous imagery of the Western Church. Hieratic figures face the beholder and gaze at him fixedly, often from the corners of their eyes, in such a way that they gain, above all in candlelight, an inexplicable semblance of life. Such paintings could not fail, together with the magnificent hymns and solemn liturgical processions, to impress a people standing on the threshold of a new age and gifted with a large measure of artistic sensibility, and we shall see that the Russians created imperishable masterpieces in that field. Like all other peoples that embraced Byzantine Christianity in the Middle Ages, they realized that an icon was essentially both devotional image and work of art. In order to do justice to this twofold function we shall not only draw attention to the religious content of the icons, but also show how that content changed in the course of their art-historical development. We shall confine our survey to the Old Russian period, the twelfth to the seventeenth century, and conclude with a brief reference to the final phase in the eighteenth century – the same limits that are applied in the study of Old Russian literature, a subject closely related to icon painting.

The specific character of icons is reflected in their formal qualities. The Byzantine iconoclasts of the eighth and ninth centuries had been opposed by theologians who followed the Church Fathers in maintaining that sacred images used in the service of God were also works of art – just as the singing of chants was justified by the Byzantine hymnologists. The reasoning that led the defenders of icons to connect the liturgical significance of an image with its intellectual and aesthetic aspects is still of interest. According to their arguments, what is represented in an icon is to be regarded as a true copy or likeness (in Greek: *eikon*) of its prototype, in an analogical sense. Naturally this view came to influence the structure of the composition. Hence, for instance, the arrangement of subjects within a picture could take the form of a view from above, which eliminates overlapping and so enables us to recognize all persons and objects depicted. This type of perspective, to take one example, allows us to look into the bowl in the *Trinity* of Rublev (Plate 30) and so to see the lamb's head, which is of importance for the interpretation of this icon: the faithful are somehow drawn into the picture and enter a kind of dialogue with it – a situation characteristic of icons as a whole. Another compositional scheme makes use of relative or 'ranking' perspective; and a knowledge of it makes it easier to understand the construction and meaning of such icons as that reproduced in Plate 15. Among the formal devices was also the 'nose modulus', which was used not only to work out the proportions of head and face – the repository of the mind –, but also to draw the entire body. A study of this theory of proportions helps, for example, in analysing how Rublev differed from Dionissi in representing the human figure. Lastly it should be noted that all such formal considerations go hand in hand with a problem peculiar to the icon as a two-dimensional 'window onto eternity': the window must at the same time open towards the beholder, in order that he may enter into close communion with the spiritual content embodied in the painting. This further interplay required the painters, working within the formal framework already outlined, not to counteract, but at least to modify, the two-dimensional, poster-like effect (which is so conspicuous in the icons of Dionissi). Their principal means to that end was the illusionistic use of light and shade, and they learned to model heads and faces, but often also the costumes, with a surprising plasticity.

Icons were not introduced into Russia immediately after the 'baptism of the country'. They are not prescribed in the Church canons as an indispensable adjunct to public worship, and the high screens with their rows upon rows of icons did not yet exist. Instead, the walls and pillars of a church were covered with frescoes or mosaics, and here the faithful who came to pray and ask for intercession would find devotional images, which called for veneration (though not for adoration). The earliest icons to reach Russia came from the cultural sphere of Byzantium, and it is not surprising that the oldest of the very few survivals from the period of Kievan Rus, *Our Lady of Vladimir* (Plate 1), is of Byzantine origin. In this magnificent work the classical ideal of beauty, so greatly cherished in twelfth-century Byzantium, is joined to a close, profoundly tender bond between the Mother of God and her Child. The intimate blending of utterly unsentimental melancholy with ideal beauty embodied in recognizable form is designed to lead the faithful into the mystery of the Incarnation, of God made man. That is the purpose underlying all representations of the Virgin Mary with the Christ Child. At the same time the idea of the Incarnation was linked to the belief that the Virgin, and the celebration of her feasts, afforded protection to a church, a monastery or an entire people. One of the first Byzantine miraculous images of the Madonna of Mercy ('Umilenie'), this icon must have been painted in an imperial workshop in Constantinople towards the end of the eleventh century and reached Kiev during the first half of the twelfth century. Here it was set up as a standard in the Grand-Prince's residence. In 1155 it was taken by Andrei Bogolyubski to his newly founded city of Vladimir on the river Klyazma, and since then it has been known as *Our Lady of Vladimir*. A similar mingling of theological doctrine, artistic ideal of beauty, and belief in the Virgin's importance for the community – in the efficacy of her protection – is found in the splendid *Great Panhagia* (Plate 4), painted in Kiev during the twelfth century. The Christ Child in the medallion on her breast symbolizes the incarnation in her womb, after Isaiah 7:14: 'Behold, a virgin shall conceive, and bear a son, and shall call his name Immanuel.' As Our Lady raises up her hands (a type known as *Orans*) with a powerful gesture in a prayer of intercession, the Russian people receive the blessing of God's eternal Word. In Kievan Rus her national patronage found special expression in the feast and depiction of *The Dormition of the Virgin* ('Uspenie') (Plates 9 and 27), but this was temporarily neglected by Andrei Bogolyubski in favour of *Our Lady of Refuge and Succour* (e.g. Plate 13). In addition to Our Lady, the 'holy knights' were invoked as important guardians. One of them was St Demetrius of Thessalonica, who is shown in

Plate 3 as a captain in splendid armour, wearing a precious diadem. As the principality of Kiev was constantly harassed and devastated by raiders from the steppes, it is natural that the people attached importance to the patronage of the 'warrior saints'.

Much more peaceful themes are depicted in *Our Lady of the Monastery of the Caves* (Plate 2) and *St Michael* (Plate 5). The Archangel is shown, not in his warlike role as the captain of the angelic host, but as a heavenly deacon carrying the insignia of his authority, the sceptre in the right hand and the orb displaying the bust of the youthful Pantocrator in the left. On the other icon Our Lady is seen as guardian of the famous subterranean monastery which played a very important part in the religious, cultural, social and political life of Old Kiev and contained as its principal church the one dedicated to the feast of The Dormition of Our Lady ('Uspenie'). This icon is particularly precious because it contains the oldest surviving, strongly characterized portraits of the two founders of the monastery, St Feodossi (died 1074) on the left and St Antoni (died 1073) on the right. To signify that he practised the strictest form of ascesis, seclusion underground (in Russian 'satwornik'), Antoni wears the 'great monastic habit' or *schima*; but he has pulled the hood back from his face. Whereas *Our Lady of Vladimir* (Plate 1) had served to proclaim the Grand-Princes' sovereignty, *Our Lady of the Monastery*, with the two monks, testifies not only to the full independence of a fraternity that was often in conflict with the ruling house, but also to the veneration of all the people of Kiev.

The second city of Kievan Rus was Novgorod on Lake Ilmen, the place from which the Grand-Princes had originally moved to the sunny capital on the Dniepr. Novgorod lay on the road 'from the Varangians (roving Northmen) to the Greeks', the road on which soldiers and merchants travelled from the North to Constantinople, the famous Imperial City, in search of adventure or in pursuit of trade. The Grand-Prince of Kiev used to send one of his sons or a noble relative to govern Novgorod in his name, and some precious icons produced in the workshops attached to this court or to its monasteries have come down to us. The harmonious interlocking of religious content and pictorial configuration, the icon's function as both devotional image and work of art, is convincingly realized in the large, magnificent *Annunciation* from Ustyug (Plate 10), painted during the twelfth century. The dogma of the Incarnation, to which we have already referred, is here visually formulated in a manner such as is but rarely found in later works: above, in a visible segment of heaven, is shown the 'Ancient of Days' after Daniel 7:9, the symbol of the pre-existent Son of God, who is seen again becoming flesh in the Virgin's womb – a doubling that is comparable with the numerous pictorial variations of the Mother and Child. By combining the distinct, masklike beauty of the faces of Mary and Gabriel – a beauty such as we find also in the Angel's head in Plate 8 – with the solemn, statuary language of gesture of the ancient theatre, the artist has conveyed their dialogue situation, following Luke 1:26-28 and the hymns for the Feast of the Annunciation on 25 March. The colour scheme, with the almost ethereal hues of the Angel's garment and the Virgin's crimson cloak over the deep, rich blue of her robe – repeated in the segment above – reinforces by its clarity the intellectual rather than mystical content of the picture.

An icon typical of the way in which the painters of Novgorod interpreted the canonical themes is *The Dormition of the Virgin* (Plate 9). The lucid structure of the composition and the clear, light colouring make for a basic economy, while the expressions of the mourners are both tense and controlled, as can be seen in the face of the Apostle bending over the

Virgin's body. The painter of the icon in Plate 7 has captured the spiritual intensity that pervades the hymns of Good Friday, of other Fridays and of the Feast of the Exaltation of the Cross (14 September), in a visual formula that is equally severe, indeed almost stylized; but its rigidity is softened by the brilliant colouring and the simple patterns on the borders. The most perfect expression of invisible, purely intellectual beauty clothed in visible form is the legendary icon of the so-called '*Acheiropoietos*' or 'The Redeemer not painted by human hands' (Plate 6). Already the Byzantines tended to look upon this masklike face, inexorably facing forwards, with wide-open eyes and curiously shaped hair and beard, as a kind of second incarnation of Christ, spreading mystical terror. 'The beautiful is but the beginning of the terrible, and the limit of what we can bear.' These words of Rilke define precisely the psychological effect of this picture, which aims at fascinating the beholder, an aim quite in keeping with Byzantine artistic principles. An intermediate stage between this approach and a very different one can be seen in the two-sided icon reproduced in Plates 11 and 12. *St Paraskyeva*, invoked in Old Russia as patron saint of household management and commerce, shows clear stylistic echoes of the works just discussed, but *Our Lady of the Sign* (displaying a medallion with the Saviour), with her mild expression, her butterfly eyebrows and fine eyelashes, together with the light boyish face of the pre-existent Christ in the medallion, suggests a reaction to the trends prevalent in Byzantine art.

The icons of the Novgorod School are distinguished by a lucid, almost rational organization of long-established iconographic schemes, by transparent, brilliant colours, a striving for naturalism and an avoidance of exaggerated formality. These painters rejected the mystical cave of Byzantine art, with its subdued, indirect light, in favour of the bright, natural spontaneity of a direct religious sensibility. One of the best examples is the icon of *Our Lady of Refuge and Succour* ('Pokrov') reproduced in Plate 13, a theme originating in Vladimir-Suzdal and glorifying the Virgin as protector of the nation. In a manner reminiscent of Plate 9, a complex ritual ceremony is here made clear by means of horizontal articulation. Christ blesses the Virgin's protective mantle, which Angels are stretching over her and over those assembled round her. At the right of the royal door, Andrew, the 'Fool in Christ', asks his servant: 'Do you behold the Queen who reigns over the world?' All have gathered under the brilliant blue roofs and cupolas of the Cathedral of St Sophia in Novgorod. Another icon of the fourteenth century is the peculiar, anthropomorphic representation of the Trinity, *The Divine Fatherhood* (Plate 14), which attempts to make the Three Persons of the One God visible in the forms of the Ancient of Days (whom we have already seen in Plate 10), the youthful Christ, and the Dove of the Holy Ghost (see also the remarks to Plate 30). The pictorial formulation addresses itself to the intellect, and this rational approach is supported by a colour scheme based on red, blue-grey, white and light brown tones, and is reinforced by the pillar-saints at the sides and the seraphim on the back of the mighty throne. The strange iconography of this picture had its origin probably in the Balkans.

The merchant city of Novgorod was not only the window through which medieval Russia looked out on the West: it also ruled over an enormous colonial territory extending as far as the shores of the Arctic Ocean. Hence it is not surprising that patron saints of fields, forests, herds and commerce were shown in the Novgorod icons not as remote figures, but rather as partners of the people. St George, the great protector of peasants and their flocks, but also a friend of the grey wolf, was invoked as the bringer of heavenly light, and also, having slain the dragon threatening order and society, as the civilizer of the waste forests in the far North of Russia. His fight with the dragon is here depicted on two icons. In one of them, painted in delicate tints (Plate 21), the encounter is set before the complicated, yet graceful architecture of a city and is watched by the princess and her parents. This picture was probably painted in Pskov. The other, which comes from the Vologda (Plate 22), shows the silhouette of a North Russian wooden house, with the entire family assembled on the roof. St George also appears, together with St Vlassi, the protector of cattle, on an early icon (Plate 15): both figures are close to the soil and look up, from the corners of their eyes, to a third Saint, who towers over them to the distant heights of heaven: he is St John called 'The Ladder' (climax), an early ascetic. Red was a favourite colour of the icon painters of Novgorod and Northern Russia, and it dominates also the colour scheme of *Elijah's Ascent to Heaven in the Fiery Chariot* (Plate 24), painted during the sixteenth century. This Old Testament prophet, too, was invoked as a powerful patron of peasants, and in particular he was believed to have influence over the weather. The way in which his disciple Elisha tries to hinder his teacher from leaving the earth may suggest something of the medieval Russian peasant's deep attachment to one of his most popular protectors. St Paraskyeva, the figure symbolizing Good Friday, whom we have seen in Plate 12 as patron of commerce, appears in a tranquil, rigidly frontal pose on another icon (Plate 20), together with St Gregory of Nazianzus called the Theologian, St John Chrysostom, and St Basil the Great. The contrast between the lively patterns on the liturgical vestments of the three Church Fathers and the muted rendering of her cloak and robe lends this work a special charm.

Other themes and motifs, too, were given quite individual interpretations by painters working in and around Novgorod. The painter of the icon reproduced in Plate 16 varied the type we have seen in Plate 6, taking over the motif of the wide-open eyes, but treating the face, the hair and the beard, as well as the highlights, distinctly in the manner of a draughtsman. The peculiar pointed beard has earned the picture the byname '*The Redeemer with the moist beard*'. Two icons relating to feast days of the Orthodox church calendar are of extraordinary artistic quality. On a fifteenth-century icon of *The Transfiguration* (Plate 17), a Biblical event commemorated on 6 August, Christ is shown in his white raiment before an aureole shimmering in various shades of blue. The remarkable brilliance of the soft colouring matches the elegance of the figures. Some of the details suggest that the painter, or those who ordered the icon, must have been acquainted with the visionary, ascetic Hesychast movement of the time (see the remarks to Plate 28). One of the finest icons celebrating the Feast of Easter, *Christ's Descent into Hell* from Vologda (Plate 23), dates from the end of the fifteenth century. Christ, triumphant over the powers of darkness, tramples the crushed gate-post of Hell underfoot. He is being adored by Adam, the Prophets of the Old Testament and St John the Baptist on the left and by Eve and the Apostles on the right, while Death and the Devil are being tormented and imprisoned in the lowest depths of the underworld. The clear, somewhat frosty colouring recalls the North Russian landscape shortly before sunrise on a late winter day in March or April, the time of the festival. The unique brilliance of the transparent colours accords very felicitously with the Orthodox Easter message: 'The Day of the Resurrection, let us become Light, ye nations.'

Novgorod icons had one special feature in common with Western religious art: the painters were not averse to depicting scenes from the history of their city and from contemporary life. One example is the large icon of *The Defence of Novgorod against the Troops of Suzdal* (Plate 18), which shows a dramatic event of the twelfth century. This 'history picture' combines all the features of colouring, style and composition which we have already mentioned. In the top register the icon of 'Our Lady of the Sign' (see Plate 11) is being carried in procession from the Church of the Transfiguration across the bridge spanning the river Volkhov to the Cathedral of St Sophia in the Novgorod Kremlin. In the middle register the icon, as guardian of the city walls, withstands a shower of arrows. Finally, in the bottom register it guides, as 'bringer of victory', the successful counter-attack of the soldiers of Novgorod, led by such national patrons as Alexander Nevski, Boris and Gleb, against the faltering enemy troops, those in the rear already turning to flight. The colours are bright and cheerful. In contrast *The Vision of the Sacristan Tarassi* (Plate 19) is painted in sombre tones, appropriate to the subject: the destruction of this proud city, while above, in a complex crowd composition, the heavenly hosts gather round the image of the Virgin and St John the Baptist interceding with Christ (known as *Deësis*) in the centre. The strong reds, formerly so exhilarating in the colour symphonies of Novgorod art, have now become symbolic of an apocalyptic catastrophe, which is shown with a wealth of terrifying incidents. Streets and houses are rendered with topographic precision, as the sacristan, clinging to his ladder, looks upon the imminent end of his city. During the same century in which this large icon was painted, the independence of Novgorod was finally brought to an end, in January 1570, by the bloodthirsty soldiery of Tsar Ivan the Terrible.

Meanwhile Kievan Rus had collapsed in the thirteenth century under the onslaught of the Mongols. In the wake of that disaster the Grand-Princes of Moscow undertook the enormous task of 'recovering the soil of Russia' under the constant threat of raids by ravaging Tartars. The national effort was strongly supported by the Church, and icons, too, were given a special part to play. Now they became more than aids to spiritual edification: they also demonstrated that the people, longing for liberation from the Tartar yoke, endorsed the policy of the rulers. This very important function of confirming the identity of the popular aspirations with those of the Grand-Princes was fulfilled by pictures dealing with old and new devotional themes in a style determined by the growing self-confidence of the rising central power of Moscow. Two sons of the Grand-Prince Vladimir of Kiev, Boris and Gleb, murdered in 1015 during an internecine feudal war, had been canonized shortly afterwards as the first national patron saints and guarantors of the 'unity of the Russian country'. Apart from a brief interruption during the reign of Andrei Bogolyubski of Vladimir-Suzdal, their cult flourished and was eagerly promoted by the Grand-Princes of Moscow. The magnificent icon of the two brothers (Plate 25), with its contrasting and matching reds as symbols of their martyrdom and its resplendent princely costumes, is striking evidence of artistic means adapted to new ends: the favourite colour of the Novgorod painters, who were averse to every unnecessary display, has here been put to the service of a ruling group which, on the contrary, set great store by ecclesiastical and political pomp. Dmitri Donskoi's first victory over the Tartars, on the plain of Kulikovo on the River Don in 1380, gave rise to the legend that an icon of Our

Lady sent to his camp by the Don cossacks had decided the battle. The legend is associated with the icon of *Our Lady of the Don* (Plate 26), which later accompanied several Grand-Princes and Tsars on their campaigns, among them Ivan the Terrible, when he defeated the Tartars at Kazan in 1552. It reverts to the old theme of *Our Lady of Vladimir* (Plate 1), but the tender intimacy of Mother and Child is now even closer. The dynamic treatment of the traditional iconographic scheme and a certain subtlety in the colouring make it very likely that the icon is from the hand of the great Theophanes, a painter from Greece (in Russian: 'Feofan Grek'). *The Dormition of the Virgin* on the reverse (Plate 27) is definitely to be attributed to him, and if we compare its composition with that in Plate 9 we cannot fail to be struck by the extraordinary concentration on essentials with which the artist conceived and designed this 'summary' of a very old theme. He has avoided the danger of lapsing into stylized formulas by accentuating the intensity of the expressions and by the telling choice of colours. In Theophanes' *Transfiguration* (Plate 28) gestures and facial expressions responding to a variety of emotions have been elaborated with the utmost care; and the excentric discs of the aureole behind Christ are remarkable. That work is of an earlier date than the fine Novgorod icon of the same subject (Plate 17) and reveals a somewhat different conception of Hesychast teaching. This monastic movement focused on the notion that the energies of the Godhead can become perceptible to human sight in visions such as that vouchsafed to the disciples watching Christ's transfiguration on Mount Tabor (Luke 9:28-36). Theophanes conveys this notion by means of a strongly dynamic and expressive style; in the serene icons of his younger contemporary, the Russian monk Andrei Rublev (about 1370–1430), it was to mature and to find its perfect pictorial realization.

Rublev grew up in the Monastery of the Trinity founded at Zagorsk in the fourteenth century by the great reformer and mystic, St Sergius. Here a harmonious combination of strict self-discipline with learning and culture had created a unique intellectual atmosphere, and he came to understand how man's ability to experience intangible, transcendental beauty was founded in God's incarnation in Christ, and how that ability had found expression in the Orthodox liturgy, in the writings of the Church Fathers, and in the lives of the Saints. The few surviving authentic icons from his hand are distinguished by that characteristic union of artistic sensibility and religious experience which manifests itself whenever the spiritual life assumes clear and severely simple forms.

This intellectual foundation of Rublev's art bore fruit in his icon of *The Redeemer* (Plate 29). The slim, noble face, based on the 'nose modulus', lacks all trace of sentimentality even for modern eyes, when they meet the forceful look of Christ directed obliquely at them. This look no longer fascinates by terrifying (see the remarks to Plate 6) in the experience of transcendental beauty; instead it may have something of the loving severity of the elders to whom the cure of souls was entrusted in Old Russia. Two distinctive traits in Rublev's style are a cautious playing down of Theophanes' 'expressionism' and a fully developed spatial illusionism. His modelling in light and shade seems to endow the figures, and particularly the faces, with the subtlest suggestion of solidity, and contrasts strongly with the precisely placed, but somewhat 'dry' hatching that the Greek master had used to indicate highlights. That notable technique alone enabled Rublev to clothe ideal concepts not accessible to the senses in a concrete form with a plasticity not achieved by any later artist. He employed the same technique in the icon of *St Paul* (Plate 31), where the somewhat abrupt foreshortening of the right half of the face and the inclination of the head with the lump on the forehead take into account the placing of the icon high on the screen, above the heads of the faithful. The colour scheme of blue, brown, red, and light purplish tones creates an effect of unobtrusive solemnity.

All the qualities that make Rublev's mastery unique and his work unmistakable are united in *The Holy Trinity* (Plate 30). This icon has come to be acknowledged throughout the Christian world as a testimony to the artistic achievement of medieval Russia, and may be said to have acquired ecumenical significance as a devotional image. And justly so, because a transcendental concept is here matched by an artistic representation of utmost economy and pellucid beauty. That concept centres on the Christian definition of the Trinity, the dogma that the One God exists in Three distinct and co-equal Persons, Father, Son, and Holy Ghost. The iconography of the Trinity had long been based on the three Angels who visited Abraham (Genesis 18: 1-16), whereas the anthropomorphic type seen in Plate 14 was much younger. But the theological interpretation of Rublev's icon is still in dispute. The fact that the painter has placed the Angels in a circle, the amazing subtlety with which he has made their incorporeality accessible to human vision, the manner in which he has conveyed the identity of their Substance through a common transparent beauty, but their distinctness through the complex colour symbolism of their garments – all this goes to emphasize the unity of the Godhead. Although the theologian in Rublev can hardly have regarded the mutual relations between the Divine Persons as a matter of little consequence, his principal aim was to stress the significance of the Trinity for the salvation of mankind. That is why he has included the bowl with the head of the lamb (John 1:29: 'Behold the Lamb of God'), both of which refer to Christ's redemptive sacrifice. According to a recent, persuasive interpretation, the Angel on the left of the picture symbolizes the Father, who is enthroned in the unapproachable light of the Godhead, the Angel in the centre the Holy Ghost sanctifying the sacrifice, and the Angel on the right the Son, reaching out his hand towards the sacrificial bowl and holding the cross formed by the staff and the upper fold of his green cloak. The blue common to the garments of all three Angels points to the single Substance of the Godhead. The artistic and aesthetic appreciation of this icon and the analysis of its symbolism will certainly continue to occupy students for a long time to come. The complexities of its figure composition and colour scheme, which are yet absorbed in a unifying classic simplicity, reflect to a far greater extent than is commonly realized the complex social and political events of the artist's day.

The second half of the fifteenth century was marked by a rise of political authority and cultural flowering under Tsar Ivan III (died 1505). But at the same time heresies were springing up and the fall of Constantinople to the Turks added to the general unrest sweeping the country. All these influences went to shape the next period of Old Russian icon painting, which was dominated by an artistic personality as outstanding as Rublev had been: the painter Dionissi (born about 1450, died before 1508). Although he regarded himself as a follower of the great master and studied his works carefully, his own approach differed in many important respects. To begin with, Dionissi was not a monk, but a layman, and this remained not without influence upon his work. In it we can discern for the first time a certain inner detachment, albeit slight and barely perceptible, not from the Christian faith, but from its doctrinal formulations. He also maintained an independent attitude towards his patrons, who supported diverse ecclesiastical factions. The deepening spiritual quality already noticeable in Rublev's work was now given fresh scope by Dionissi, and it was not without good reason that his contemporaries dubbed him 'the Ponderer'. His magnificent fresco cycles in the Therapont Monastery were didactic and devotional at the same time. There, in the elongated, inward-looking figures, the artist seems to ponder and explore the interplay of the theological dogmas they enshrine with the quite individual way in which these dogmas are viewed by the very persons representing them – a novel and distinctive approach, contrasting strongly with the way in which earlier icon painters had visualized the sacred figures as self-sufficient personalities. Dionissi joins this sensibility – not to be mistaken for sentimentality – to an astoundingly deep artistic intellect: in his work the light colour scale and the 'incorporeal corporeality' of Rublev are often intensified until they merge in an over-subtle formula, which is realized not in pictorial space, but more readily in flat patterns. *'In Thee rejoices all Creation'* (Plate 33) is a fine example of these distinctive traits. It does not lack a certain poster-like flatness, but it is painted in brilliant colours, which provide an equivalent to that jubilant Marian hymn in the Liturgy of St Basil. The Virgin, holding the Child on her lap, is surrounded by Angels and Archangels. Her head is at the centre of a wide circle, which encompasses and at the same time symbolizes the world of creation and the Church. Ecclesiastical dignitaries, saints, ascetics, men, women, and a child, assembled below, look up to her while they are chanting the hymn in her praise. The five cupolas and some other details identify the great Cathedral of the Dormition in the Moscow Kremlin. The Virgin of the Dormition had long been invoked as a patron of the nation and was accorded special veneration during the reign of Ivan III. The colour scheme suggests that the artist had absorbed the best traditions of the School of Novgorod. There, too, plants had made their appearance in paintings and had become a popular motif.

One of Dionissi's greatest works is the icon of *The Crucifixion* (Plate 32). Christ's elongated, slightly curved body hangs on a tall cross, which has unusually thin arms. The slender figures of the bystanders, three mourning women and the Virgin on the left and the beloved disciple John with the centurion on the right, likewise reinforce the dominant compositional thrust: a rising aloft, which signifies a passing from the realm of Death – symbolized by the grave of Adam at the foot of the Cross – to the bright heights of life. This idea is in keeping with the tenets of the Eastern Church, according to which Christ's death on the Cross was itself already the victory over death. One of the Orthodox hymns enshrines this belief in the words: 'Rejoice, O Cross, vessel of life; rejoice, O Cross, treasure of life.' The incorporeal Angels tremble at the sight of the Crucified, but they also, hovering at either side of his bent head, adore him with veiled hands. Below the left arm of the Cross, an Angel leads Ecclesia (the personified Church) so that she may adore the Redeemer, while on the right another drives off the Synagogue, who turns round pathetically to look once more at the Cross. This motif, which is not found elsewhere in Orthodox iconography, invests the traditional pictorial scheme with a certain ambivalence of emotion. The lyrical treatment of grief and tragedy prepares the sorrowing Christian for the mighty Easter message, as it is represented in *Christ's Descent into Hell* (Plate 23). Such barely perceptible nuances, such profound meditations upon the Good Friday imagery, are characteristic of Dionissi's personality.

The icon of *St Nicholas and Scenes from his Life* (Plate 34), which betrays certain influences of Greek iconography, was painted very probably in a Moscow workshop. An ideal portrait of the great patron in episcopal vestments is framed by the most important episodes of his life – an arrangement unlike that of *The Birth and Childhood of St Nicholas* (Plate 40), where the incidents are grouped in a single composition. The painter of Plate 34 has based his narrative on the written tradition of the saint's life and has chosen a colour scheme dominated by red and brown tones, producing an effect of great solemnity.

In the meantime the Moscow School of painting had assumed great importance to the same extent that the capital had become the nerve-centre of a strong Russian empire. In the sixteenth century Tsar Ivan IV the Terrible not only extended his domain as far as the Baltic Sea, but also began the conquest of Siberia. The fine Moscow icon depicting *Florus and Laurus*, the patron saints of horses (Plate 35), disposes them like an emblem to the left and right of the Archangel Michael. It shows a clear influence of the Novgorod School, but modified by a metropolitan refinement and piety; these account for the elegance of the figures as well as for the colour scheme, which, although it is less vivid, recalls the one seen in Plate 23.

The 'Lives of the Saints' had used literary means to present ideal portraits; icons used pictorial means to the same end. During a period of secularization in the seventeenth century the real portrait gradually made its appearance. In Plate 2 we have already seen a combination of the two types. Unlike the medieval painters in the West, the icon painters very rarely used contemporary models for sacred personages. Each of their saints had distinct, individual features, which had become standardized in the course of the centuries – in other words, the individually distinct personalities are intimately linked, in the imagination of the faithful, with their immutable prototypes. In the seventeenth century this notion was extended to persons who had not been canonized and to their icon portraits, and the resulting compromise between the style and aesthetics of the old painting and those of the new can be seen in the portrait of Prince Skopin-Shuiski (Plate 37), a young army commander, who had fought valiantly against the Polish invaders when they advanced as far as the walls of the Monastery of the Trinity and St Sergius. Although his icon is composed in flat areas, the painter now utilizes the specific technical means of his art to elaborate the distinctive features of a personality, and in doing so has taken an important step on the way from classical icon painting to a quite novel type of portraiture. This change in the depiction of individuals testifies to an equally significant change in the valuation of character. The ideal qualities of the new human type, which is found throughout the contemporary literature, are conjugal fidelity, attention to duty, and a natural humanity, which is grounded in religious principles, but often comes into conflict with the ordinances of the Church. Everyday tasks in the home and on the farm assume equal dignity before God with those in church or monastic cell. That was the time when small-size icons were given a place of honour in living rooms and so began to accompany the daily routine of the household. They came to be regarded, so to speak, as intimate friends of the family, and this change manifested itself in a new simplicity of representation. A large group of such icons has been named after the rich merchant house of the Stroganovs, and although there was never a Stroganov School in the narrower sense, the term is a convenient label, for it indicates the social environment in which these works had their origin.

Plate 36 shows St Simeon Stylites, who was said to have lived in Syria in the fifth century and to have spent forty-five years in continuous prayer on top of a pillar, which eventually rose twenty metres high. Nothing in the icon hints at the severity of this bizarre asceticism. The dizzy height of the pillar is suggested by the light clouds below the platform, the stylized background is made up of rocks, with plants growing between them. The architecture around the pillar is also stylized, and is believed to allude to the church which was built there after his death. At the top left is 'Our Lady's Corner', a very popular motif at the time. The two delightful vessels suspended on purple threads were used to supply the saint with food and drink. The delicately muted colours are cheerful rather than sombre: they must have made the faithful feel that the austere ascetic on the pillar was their comrade and partner.

This icon dates from the early years of the Stroganov School; we now turn to some of the masterpieces of the group. *Our Lady of the Monastery of the Caves, between St Nicetas and St Anastasia* (Plate 38) was painted towards the end of the sixteenth century. The theme is an old one and we have met it already in an icon (Plate 2) of the School of Kiev, which now attracted renewed interest; the treatment, however, is very typical of the new age. The figures are in the style of Dionissi, but their elongation and fragility are now overlaid with a certain elegance, and their finish suggests that the technique of miniature painting had been adapted to small icons. This is even clearer in the icon of *St Demetrius of Thessalonica with Dmitri, the son of Tsar Ivan IV* (Plate 39). The warrior saint, whom we have already seen in Plate 3, and his namesake, who was murdered as a young boy, stand below 'Our Lady of the Sign'. Both saints were much venerated by the Stroganovs, and Prokopi Tchirin, an important master, lavished great care on their portraits, particularly on the armour and the rich costumes, and on the appropriate colouring. Semeika Borozdin, another master of the Stroganov School, painted *The Birth and Childhood of St Nicholas* (Plate 40), an icon consisting of several genre scenes. The accumulation of homely incidents made this type widely popular. Legend had it that the newborn saint was able to stand for hours in a small bath-tub (bottom left) and that his mother refused to feed him on the weekly fast days (top right). Such miracles are here depicted as homely scenes of family life rather than as remote events of a distant past.

After the expulsion of the Poles from Moscow and Russia, Mikhail Romanov ascended the throne in 1613 and became the founder of a new dynasty of Tsars. In the spirit of absolute monarchy the Romanovs regarded themselves as the heirs of the Old Russian rulers and set out to crown their traditions. The painters' workshops in the Armoury Palace of the Kremlin, the 'Orusheinaja Palata', were also enlisted in the furthering of this policy. They were but one section of a large art academy, whose most important master was Simon Ushakov. His icon of *Our Lady of Vladimir: 'The Planting of the Tree of Russian Sovereignty'* (Plate 43), completed in 1668, is a classic example, both in content and structure, of the new allegorical and emblematic art. The composition adapts the traditional scheme of the genealogy of Christ, the so-called Tree of Jesse. In the centre is the medallion of Our Lady of Vladimir (Plate 1), albeit strongly sentimentalized, below a protective mantle, which two Angels spread out over her at the command of Christ. In the branches are smaller medallions with portraits of eminent Russian saints, ascetics, ecclesiastical dignitaries, Grand-Princes and Tsars. The root of the tree is being planted and watered in the Cathedral of the Dormition in the Moscow Kremlin (see also the remarks to Plate 33) by the Metropolitan Peter and the Grand-Prince Ivan Kalita, who had laid the foundation stone of the Cathedral in 1326. On their left the Tower of the Redeemer (Spasski Tower) in the Kremlin wall is clearly recognizable and at the corners stand Tsar Alexei Mikhailovitch and his family. The marked realism in the depiction of the Kremlin wall and the Uspenie Cathedral is particularly charming, and the gay colour scheme, based on subtle gradations from pink to green, strikes a note of optimism.

Simon Ushakov, a contemporary of Rembrandt, was the last great master of Russian icon painting, and with him it passed the highest point in its fascinating development. His aesthetic norms were bitterly attacked by the Archpriest Avvakum, the founder of Old Ritualism, who paid for his persistent opposition to the Patriarchate with his life: he was burnt at the stake in 1681. Avvakum championed the traditional icons with their two-dimensional style and ascetic physiognomies. Ushakov, on the other hand, sought to produce the illusion of real space and of fully rounded figures. We have noted that Rublev had, in his own way, pursued a similar aim, and indeed Ushakov studied his work and that of Dionissi with profit. He achieved ultimate perfection in suggesting plastic form by means of light and shade in the field of tempera painting. His *'Acheiropoietos'* (*The Redeemer not painted by human hands*) and particularly the youthful *Christ Immanuel* (Plates 41 and 44) repeat old motifs (see the remarks to Plates 6, 4 and 11), but Ushakov's artistic approach, with its marked sensuousness, has transformed them in a very characteristic manner. The *'Acheiropoietos'*, for instance, shows a knowledge of the sudary of St Veronica in Western art, and thus constitutes a compromise between classic Byzantine and Western prototypes. In the face of the youthful, pre-existent Christ Immanuel (Plate 44) the subtlest transitions between light and dark areas have been worked out with an extraordinary technical mastery: the painter has created an impression of tangible solidarity, and this effect extends even to such anatomical details as the throat. There is little, except the sorrowful, all-knowing glance, to connect this portrait of a boy with its age-old theological content. A comparison of the face with that of the Child of *Our Lady of Vladimir* (Plate 1) shows that Ushakov had no intention of breaking with artistic or religious traditions. But his pictorial interpretation of a transcendental concept – in this case the concept of the Redeemer's eternity and pre-existence – is basically of a surprising modernity. An example of the variety in his work is *Our Lady of Kykkos* (Plate 42), an icon painted after a Cypriot model; here he has harmoniously combined the old Byzantine approach with his own.

Another feature of the icons painted by followers of Ushakov is the introduction of landscape into the iconographic repertory. A special motif in this context is the 'Enclosed Garden' as a symbol of the Virgin Mother of Christ. In Western art the *hortus conclusus* appears first about 1400 as a motif derived from the Song of Solomon (4:12). It soon became widely popular, and the painters of the Tsar's workshop knew these pictures. The theme was familiar to them also from the Marian hymns of the Orthodox Church, but they did not begin to adopt it until they were prompted by Western painting. An icon by Nikita Pavlovets (Plate 46) shows the Virgin arrayed in gorgeous robes, holding the crowned Child, while Angels are placing a crown on her own head – yet another motif adopted from Western Madonna paintings. She is painted in flat areas, whereas the ground behind her is shown in central perspective, like a view of a contemporary garden.

The cultivated plot surrounded by a natural landscape symbolizes her theological role; one feels reminded of the icon of the Marian hymn (Plate 33), one of the earliest works in which the world of plants was associated with the glorification of the Virgin.

In several icons we have noted stylized representations of landscape or architecture, in each case serving merely as a backdrop. Now they begin to enter the pictorial stage itself and become part of the compositional structure. This important development is seen very clearly in *The Trinity with Scenes from Genesis* (Plate 45), a new version of an old subject (see the remarks to Plate 30). The schematic rocks with their upturned 'heels', derived from Byzantine art, are interspersed with plants and, more strikingly, with carefully depicted wooden houses of the Russian countryside. The real subject is the 'deeds of the Angels' after Genesis 18 and 19, and this gives the picture a markedly narrative, epic character. The problem of combining successive events in a single composition is solved by the division into two registers, in which the beholder can 'read' the Biblical text. In the upper register the Angels arrive at Abraham's house and are greeted by him; above this scene is the sacrifice of Isaac (Genesis 22). At the right of the terebinth in the plain of Mamre are the scenes from the story of Lot. In the upper right corner Lot's wife is turned into a pillar of salt. The same delight in telling a story can be seen even in the way the Holy Trinity is depicted. Rublev's classic formulation (Plate 30) had reduced the subject to its bare essentials, but our painter has again 'filled up' that model by adding redundant, 'unnecessary' motifs. For instance, he shows Sara looking out of a window of her pretty Russian farmhouse, with curiosity. However, it should not be forgotten that even early Christian artists had already invested the visit of the three Angels and Abraham's hospitality with liturgical and eucharistic significance. This underlying thought, which Rublev had formulated with the utmost economy, is here still clearly perceptible behind all the wealth of incidental motifs. The colour scheme, based on the two dominant values of green and red, gives the picture a solemn character.

The icons produced by painters attached to the Tsar's Armoury inspired many other workshops, both elsewhere in Moscow and particularly in the so-called painters' villages of Khalui and Palekh. But these influences were absorbed in a way that often combined artistic sensibility with features typical of an overripe art form. Multi-figured compositions, which had been introduced as early as the sixteenth century, now served no longer to provide a commentary to theological doctrines, but to give scope to the artist's imagination. They supplement the traditional pictorial scheme, confined to a single figure or few figures. The latter type is represented by the icon of *St John the Baptist* (or the Forerunner, as he is called in the Orthodox Church) reproduced in Plate 47. The winged image is based on hymns, which in turn derive from Malachi 3:1, Mark 1:2, and other Biblical passages, and shows him as the 'Angel revealed in the flesh' and a martyr of Christ, carrying his head, like an attribute, on a dish. At his feet, 'the ax is laid unto the root of the trees' (Matthew 3:10). There are some reminiscences of the Stroganov School in this seventeenth-century work.

Our last icon, *St John the Forerunner in the Wilderness* (Plate 48), comes from the painters' village of Palekh. The lush vegetation suggests how the painter imagined the scenery along the banks of the river Jordan, and at the same time it revives an Old Russian literary tradition, which described St John as a hermit in the forests of Russia. Below the 'Ancient of Days' (see the remarks to Plate 10), who sits enthroned in a semicircular heaven, the painter has grouped scenes from the saint's life, based on various Biblical and apocryphal sources. They are crowded with figures, and the luxuriant landscape teems with plants and animals. Inscriptions below and at the sides provide a kind of help in 'reading' the confusing composition. The fact that the icon required such a key heralds the waning of a great and profound art.

List of Plates

29. *The Redeemer*. 158 × 103·5 cm. By Andrei Rublev, about 1409. Moscow, Tretyakov Gallery.

30. *The Holy Trinity*. 141·8 × 112·7 cm. By Andrei Rublev, 1411. Moscow, Tretyakov Gallery.

31. *St Paul the Apostle*. 159 × 105 cm. By Andrei Rublev, about 1407. Moscow, Tretyakov Gallery.

32. *The Crucifixion*. 85·1 × 52·1 cm. By Dionissi, late 15th or early 16th century. Moscow, Tretyakov Gallery.

33. *'In Thee Rejoices All Creation.'* 148·5 × 110 cm. School of Dionissi, early 16th century. Moscow, Tretyakov Gallery.

34. *St Nicholas and Scenes from his Life*. 138 × 96 cm. School of Moscow, 14th to 17th century. Moscow, Tretyakov Gallery.

35. *St Florus and St Laurus*. 84·3 × 60·3 cm. School of Moscow, 16th century. Moscow, Tretyakov Gallery.

36. *St Simeon Stylites on the Pillar*. 35·4 × 28·5 cm. Early Stroganov School, 16th century. Moscow, Tretyakov Gallery.

37. *Prince Skopin-Shuiski*. 41 × 35 cm. School of Moscow, 17th century. Moscow, Tretyakov Gallery.

38. *Our Lady of the Monastery of the Caves, between St Nicetas and St Anastasia*. 36 × 30·5 cm. Stroganov School, late 16th century. Moscow, Korin Collection.

39. *St Demetrius of Thessalonica with Dmitri, the Son of Tsar Ivan IV*. 31·6 × 27·7 cm. By Prokopi Tchirin, about 1620. Moscow, Korin Collection.

40. *The Birth and Childhood of St Nicholas the Miracle-Worker*. 36 × 29·7 cm. By Semeika Borozdin, Stroganov School, 17th century. Moscow, Tretyakov Gallery.

41. *The Redeemer 'Acheiropoietos'* ('not painted by human hands'). 44·5 × 35 cm. By Simon Ushakov, 1657. Moscow, Tretyakov Gallery.

42. *Our Lady of Kykkos*. 130·5 × 76 cm. By Simon Ushakov, 1668. Moscow, Tretyakov Gallery.

43. *Our Lady of Vladimir: 'The Planting of the Tree of Russian Sovereignty'*. 104 × 61 cm. By Simon Ushakov, 1668. Moscow, Tretyakov Gallery.

44. *Christ Immanuel*. 37 × 32 cm. By Simon Ushakov, 1697. Moscow, Museum of the Novodevitshi Monastery.

45. *The Holy Trinity with Scenes from Genesis*. 133 × 127 cm. School of the Tsar's Workshop, about 1670. Moscow, Tretyakov Gallery.

46. *Our Lady: The Enclosed Garden*. 32·5 × 28·5 cm. By Nikita Pavlovets, late 17th century. Moscow, Tretyakov Gallery.

47. *St John the Forerunner*. 31 × 27·5 cm. School of Moscow, 17th century. Moscow, Korin Collection.

48. *St John the Forerunner in the Wilderness*. 31 × 26·8 cm. From the painters' village of Palekh, 18th century. Moscow, Korin Collection.

PLATES

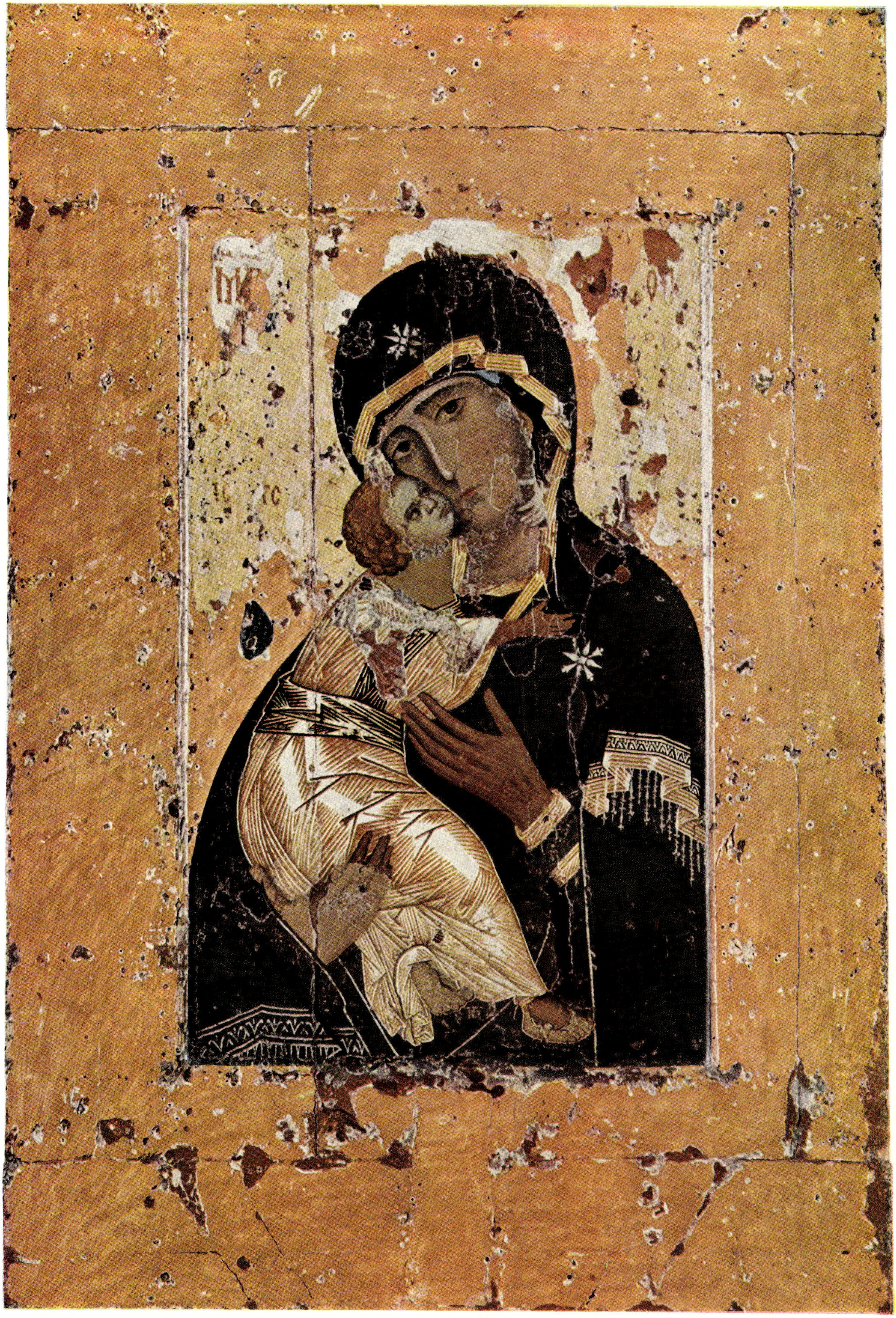

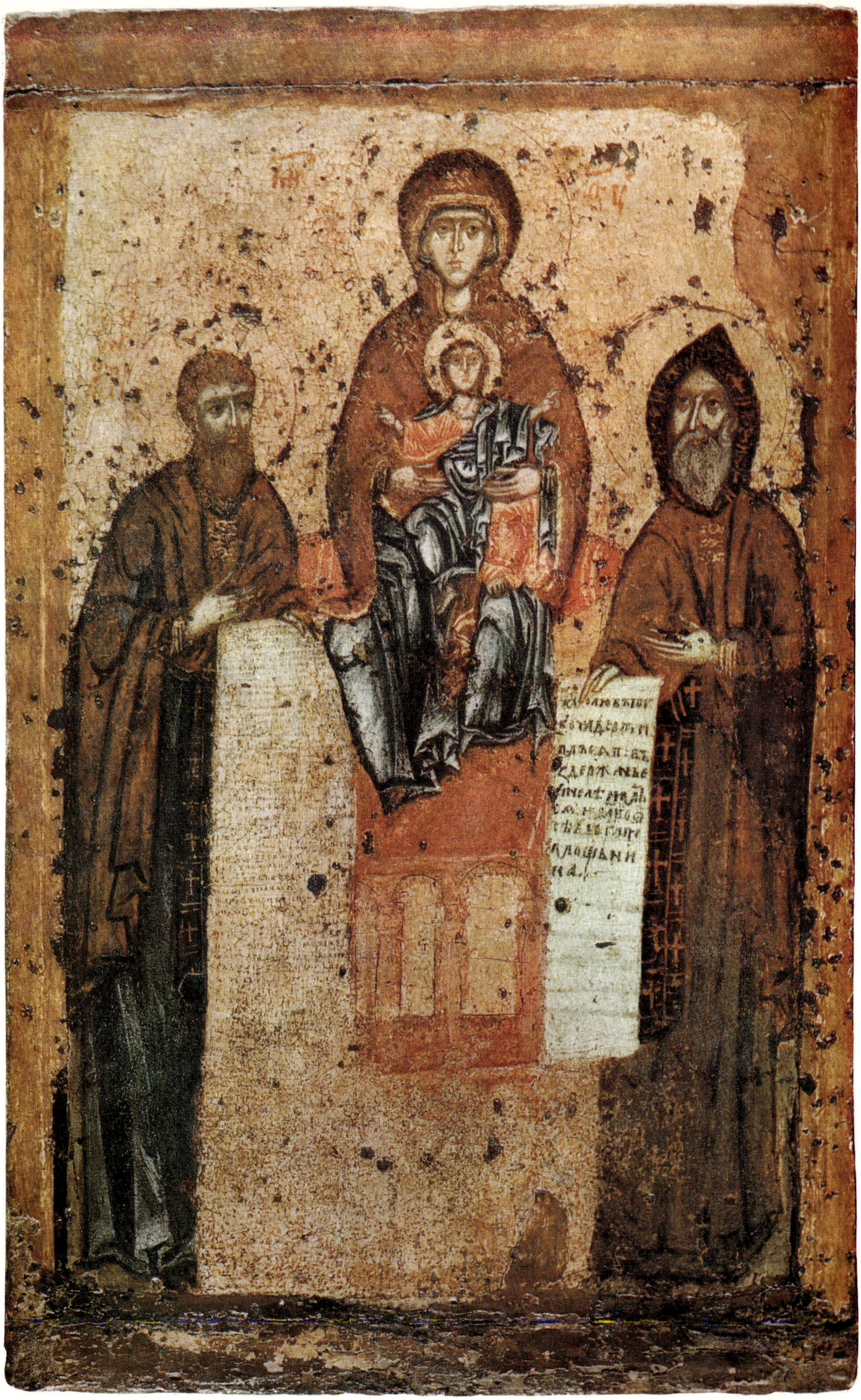

2

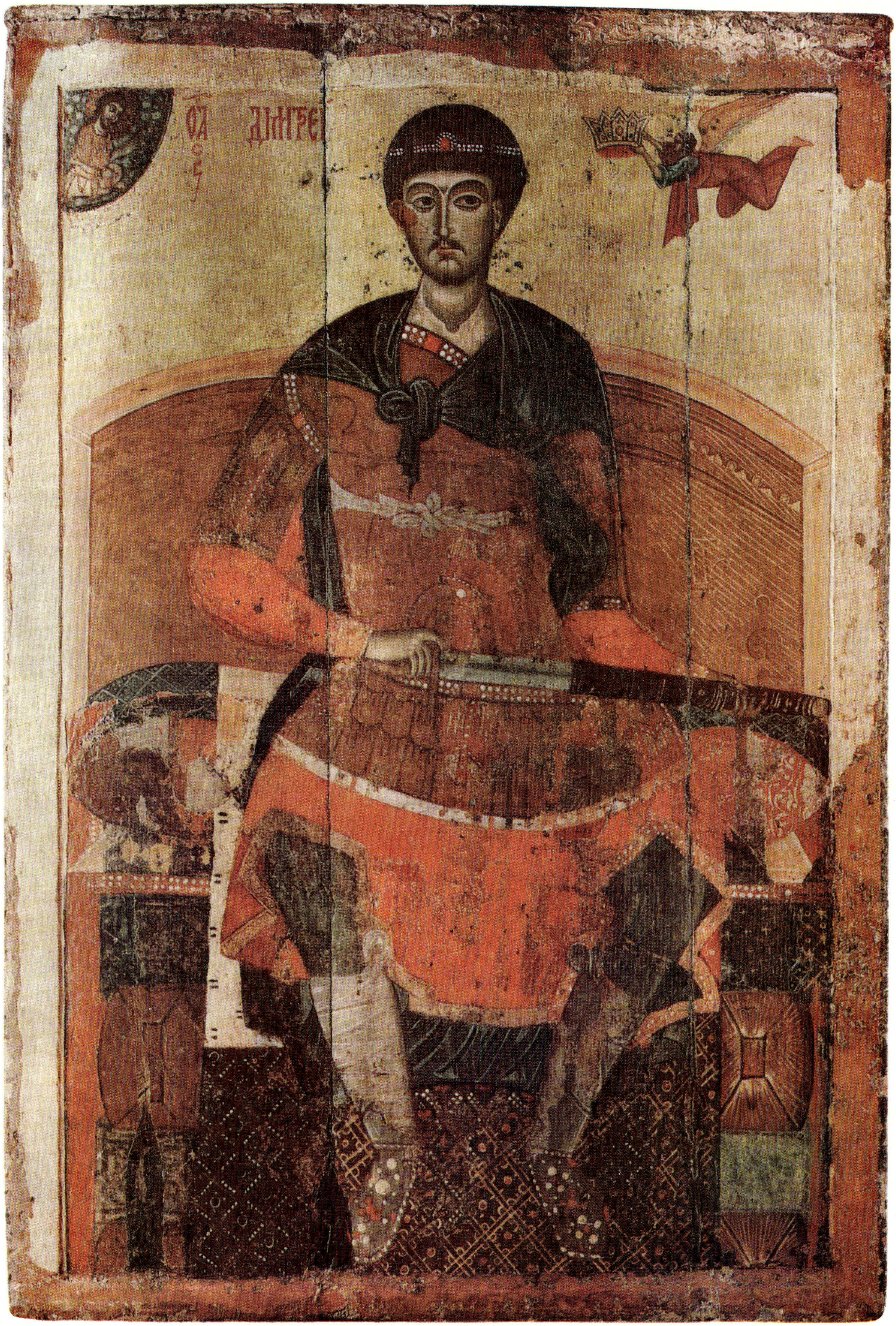

3

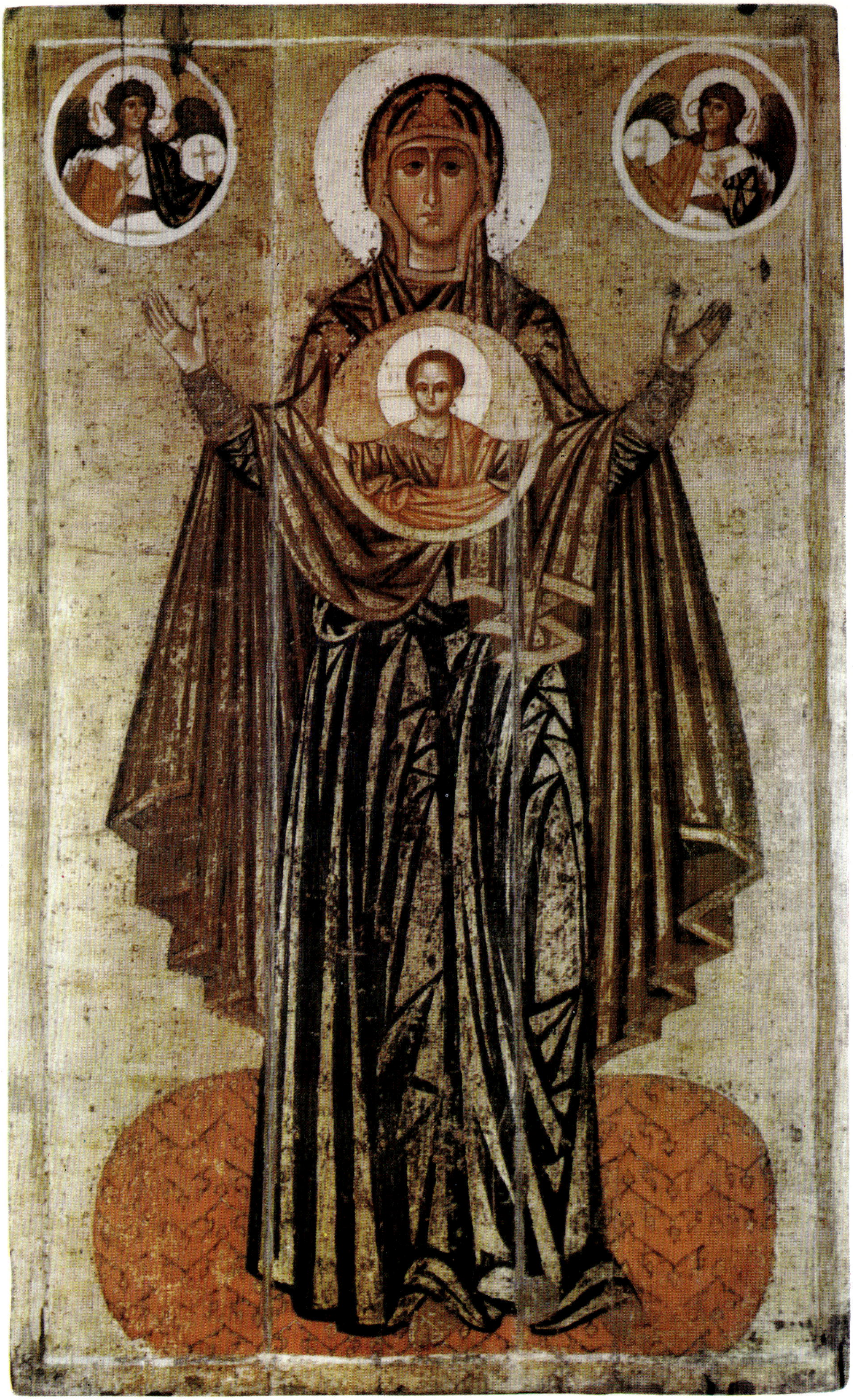

4

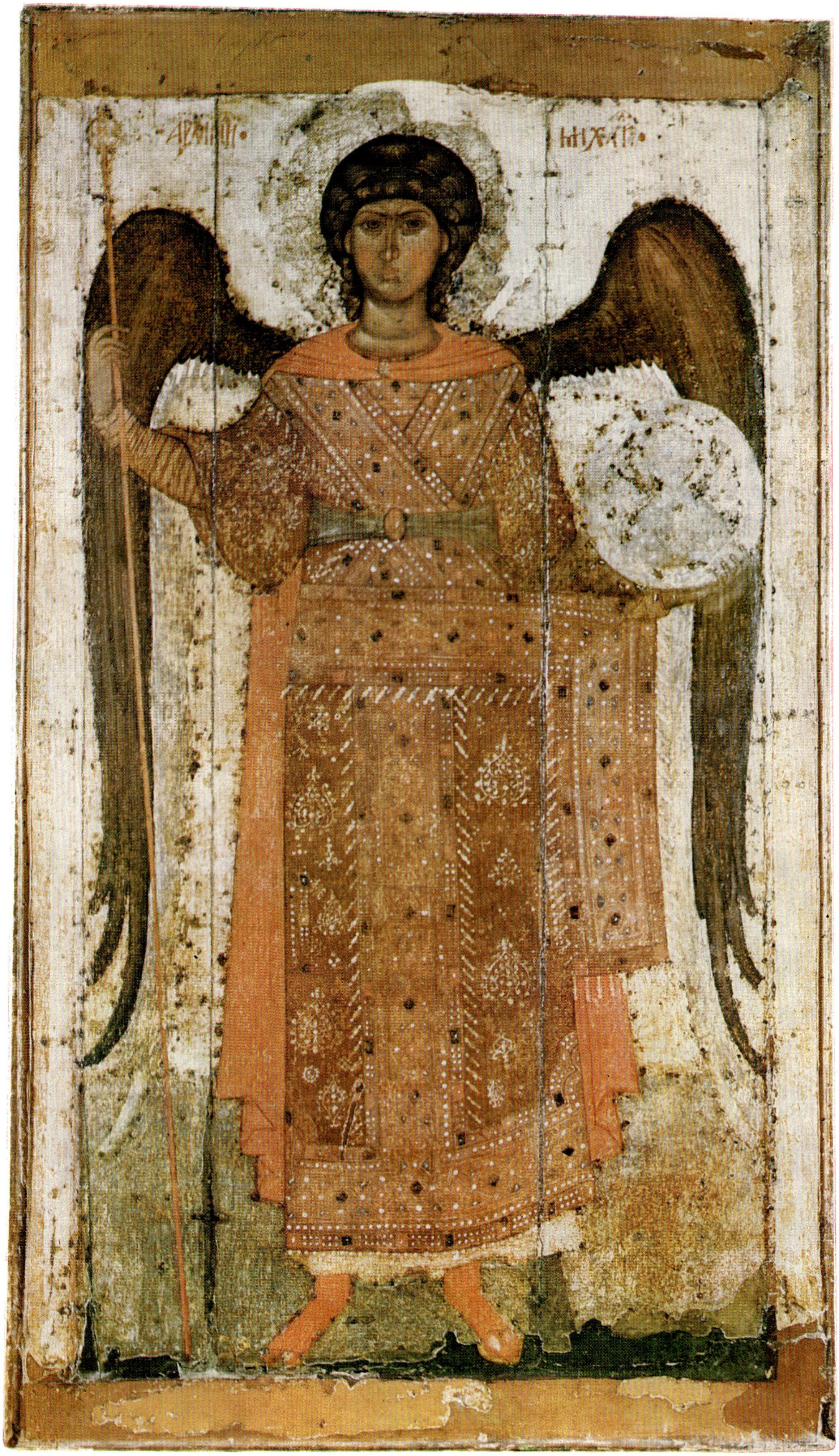

5

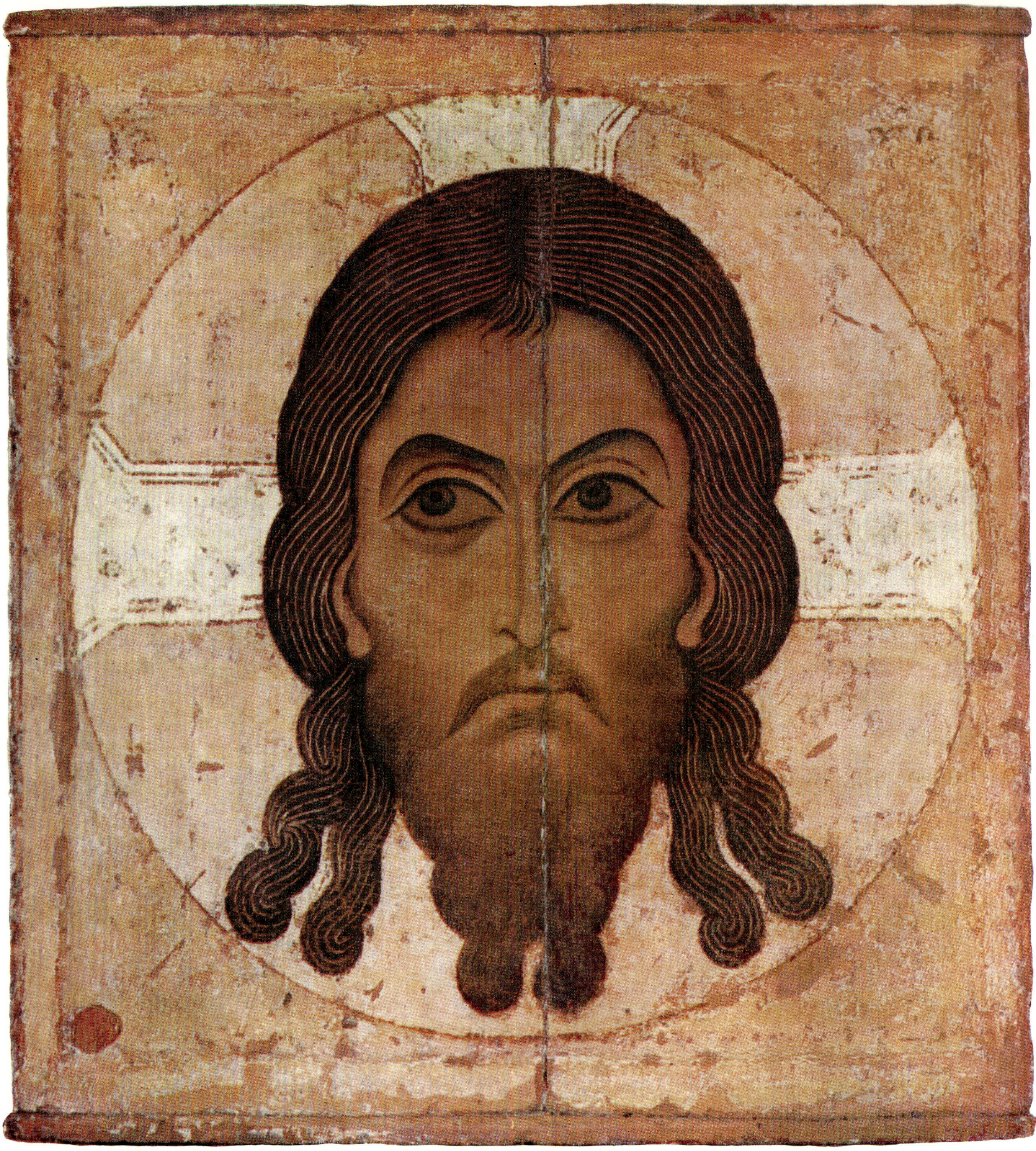

6

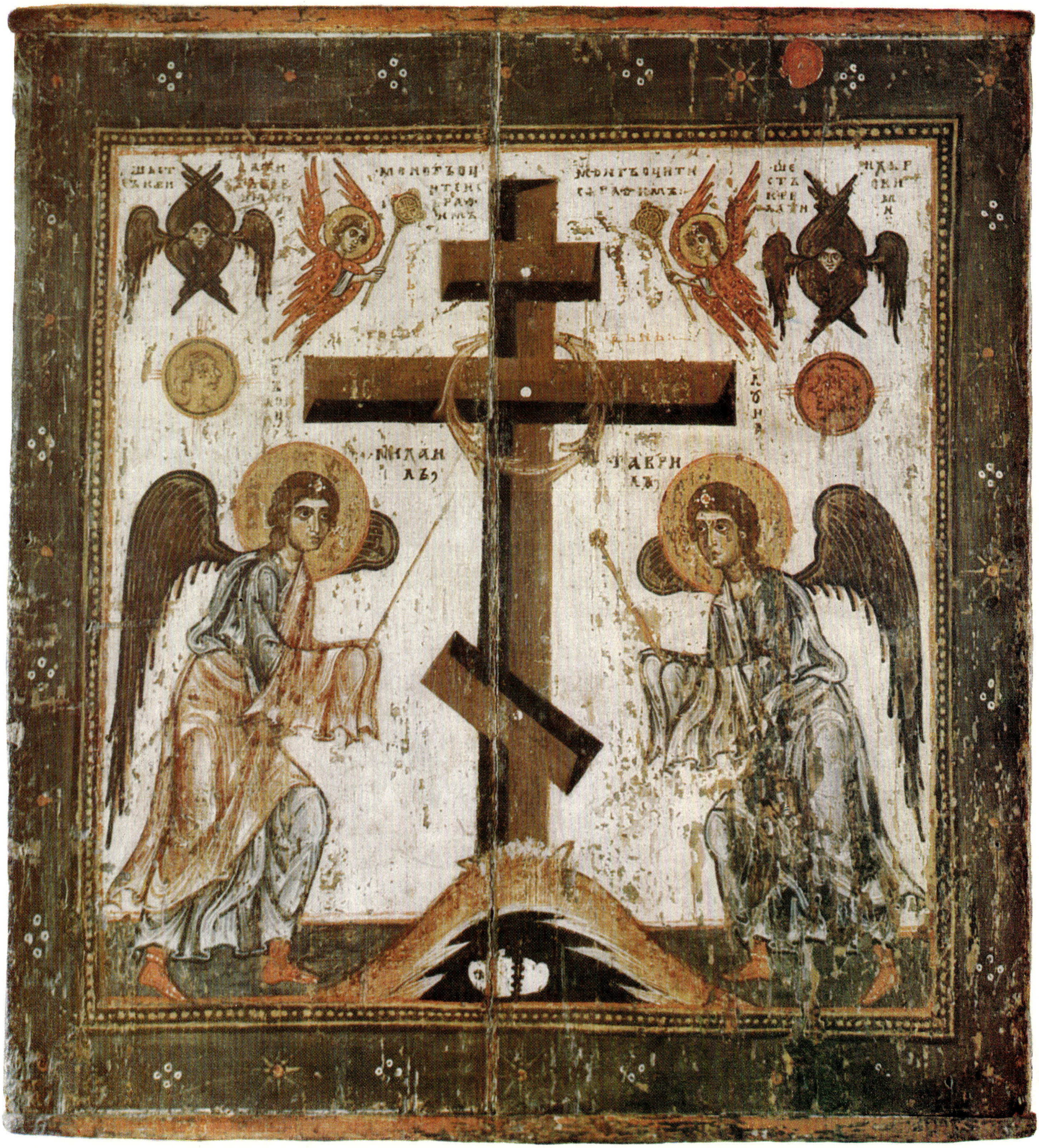

7

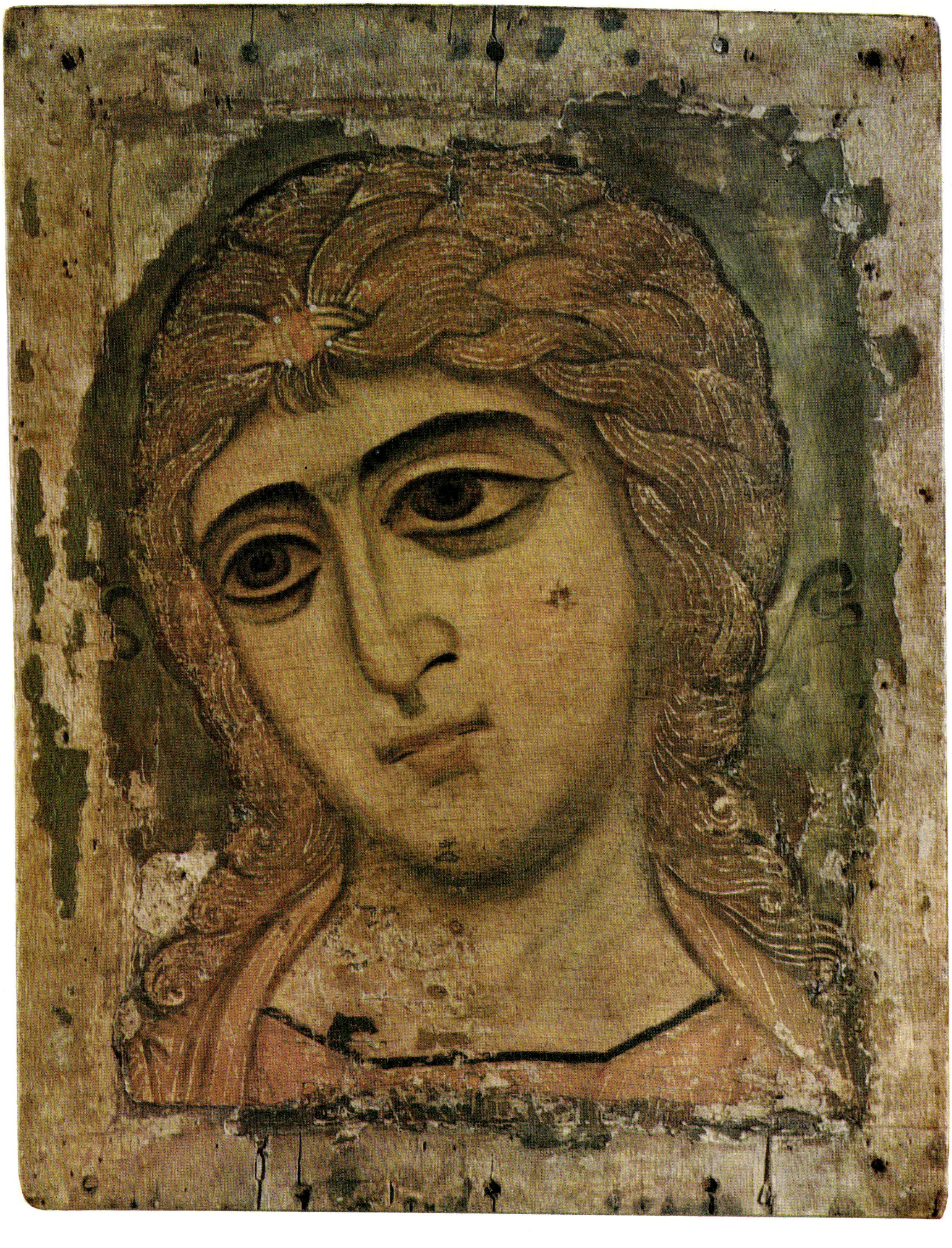

8

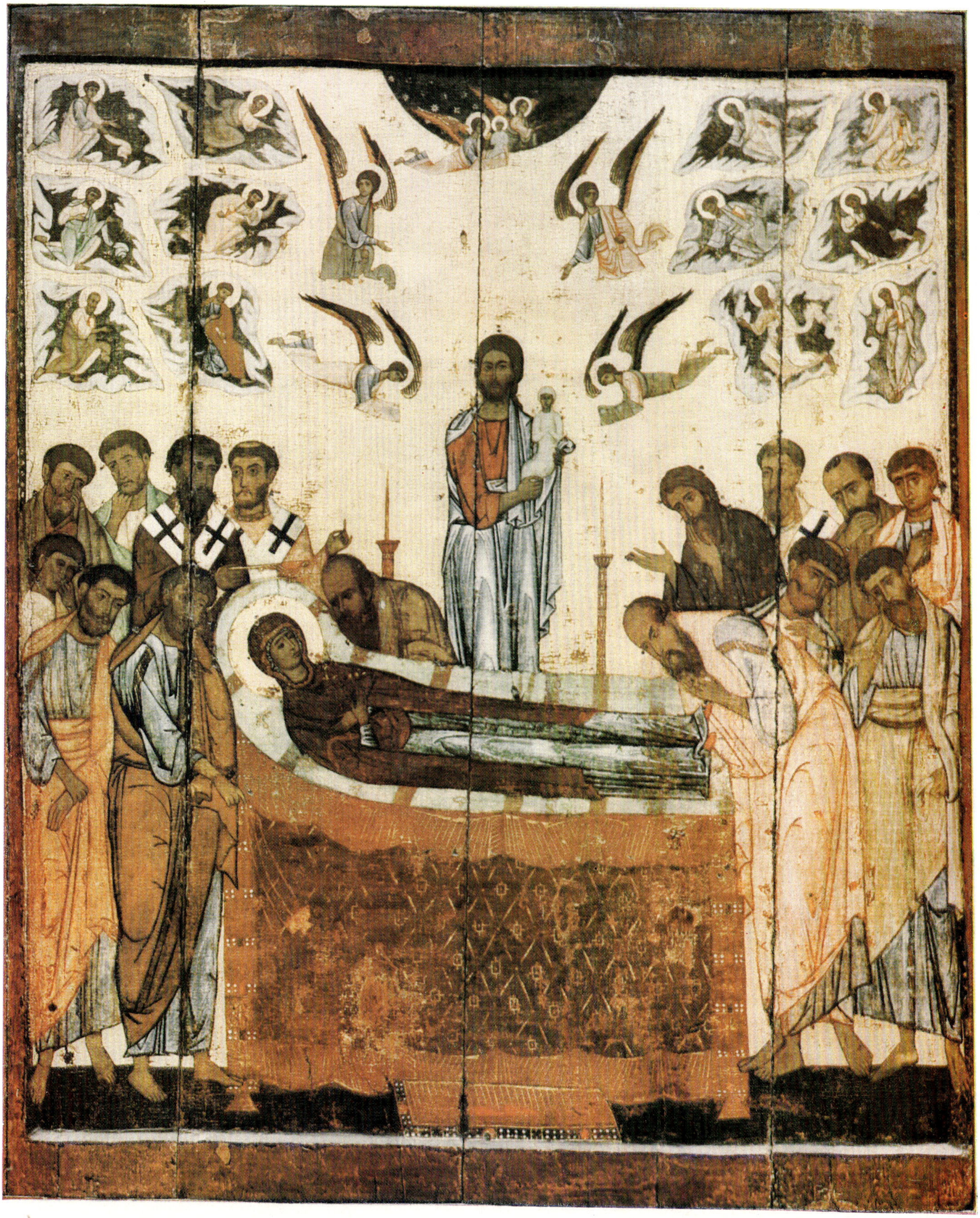

9

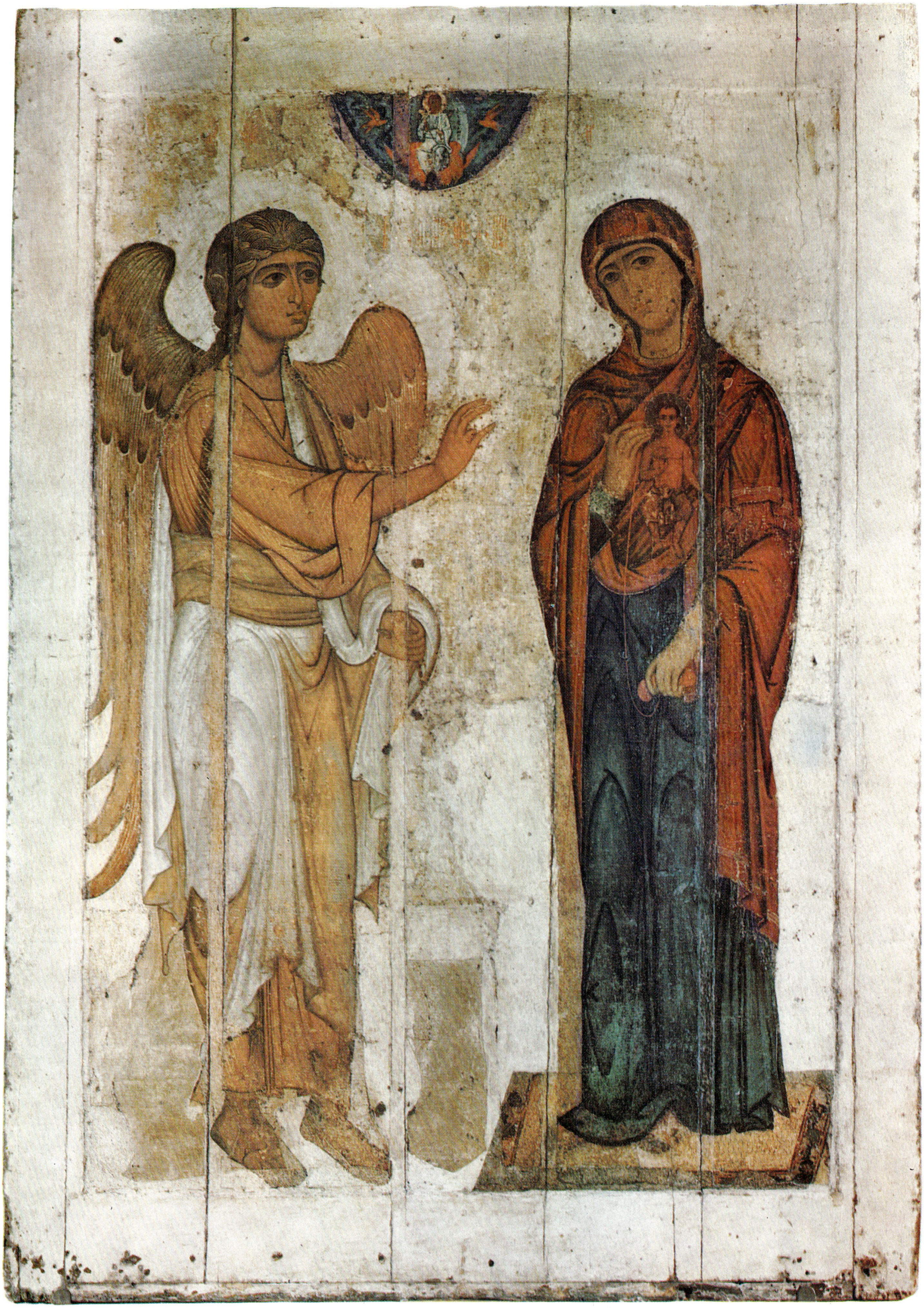

10

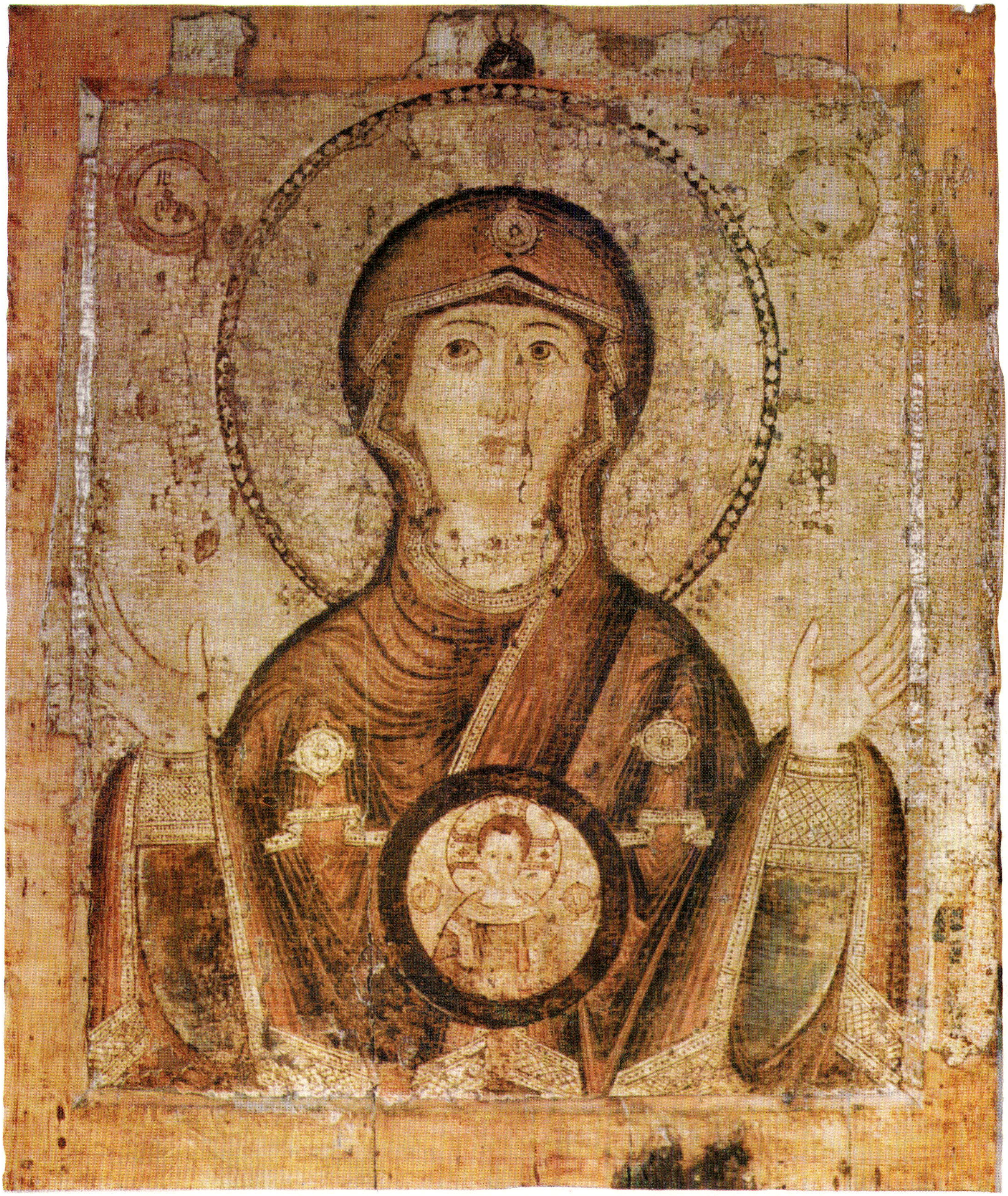

11

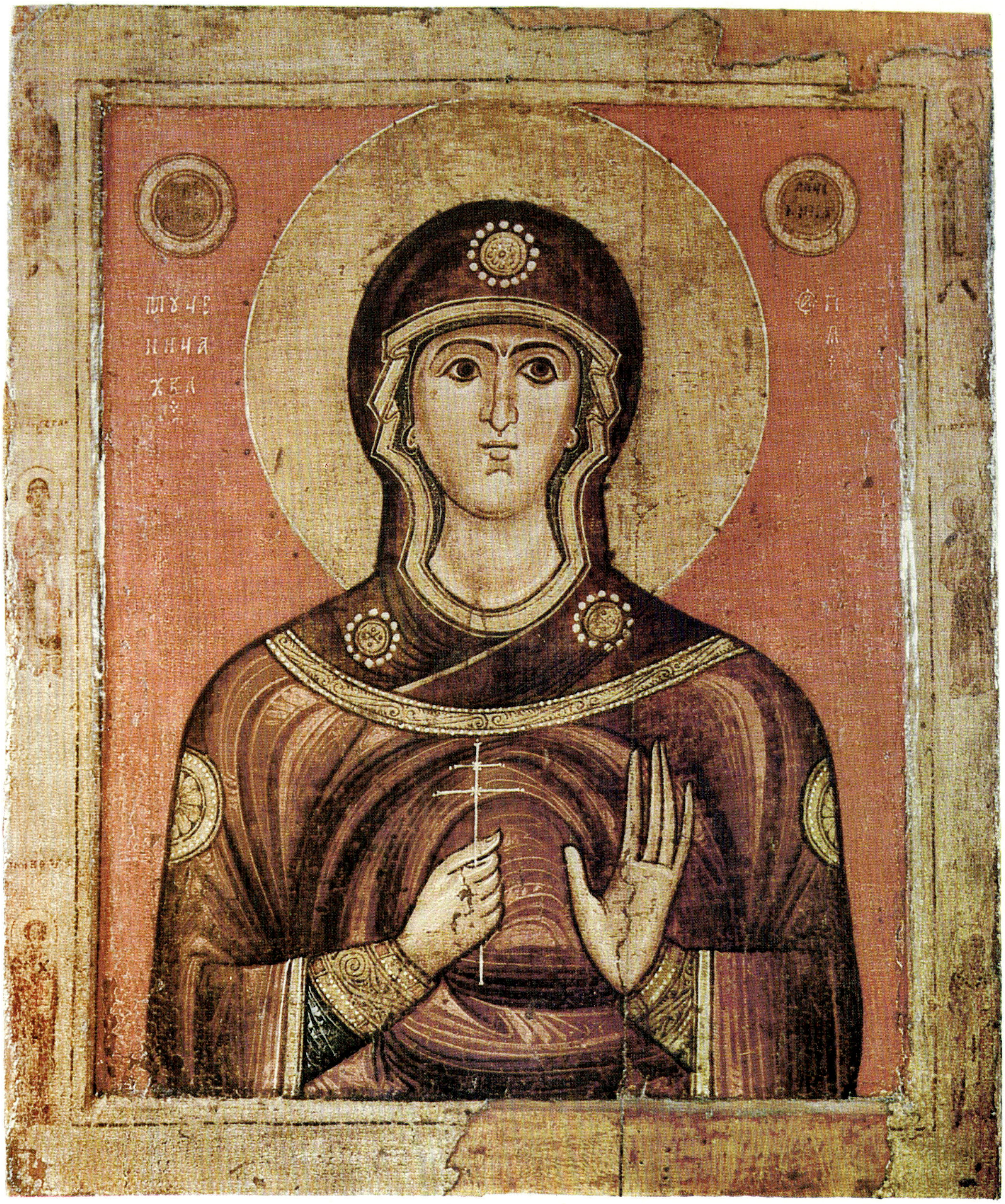

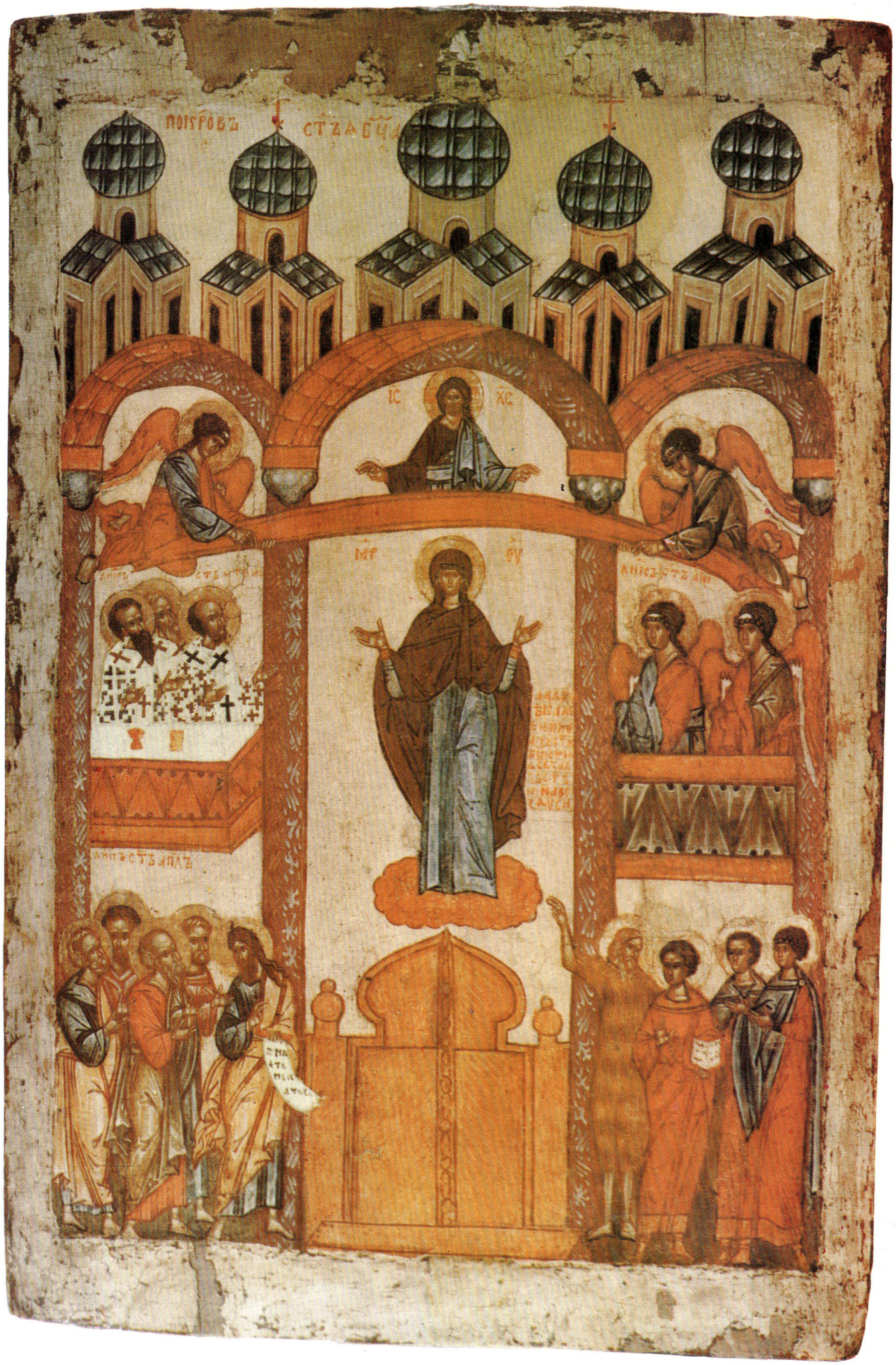

13

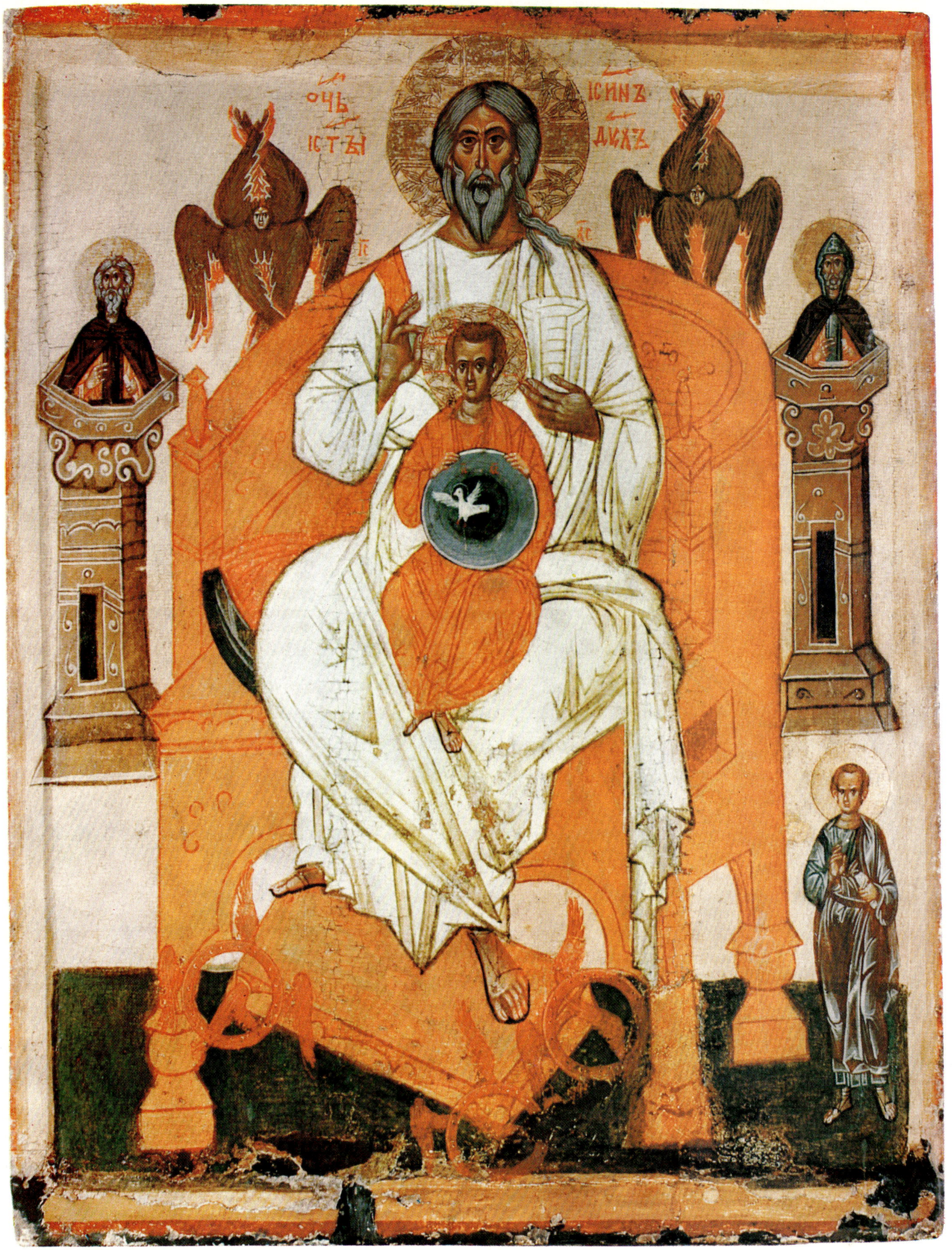

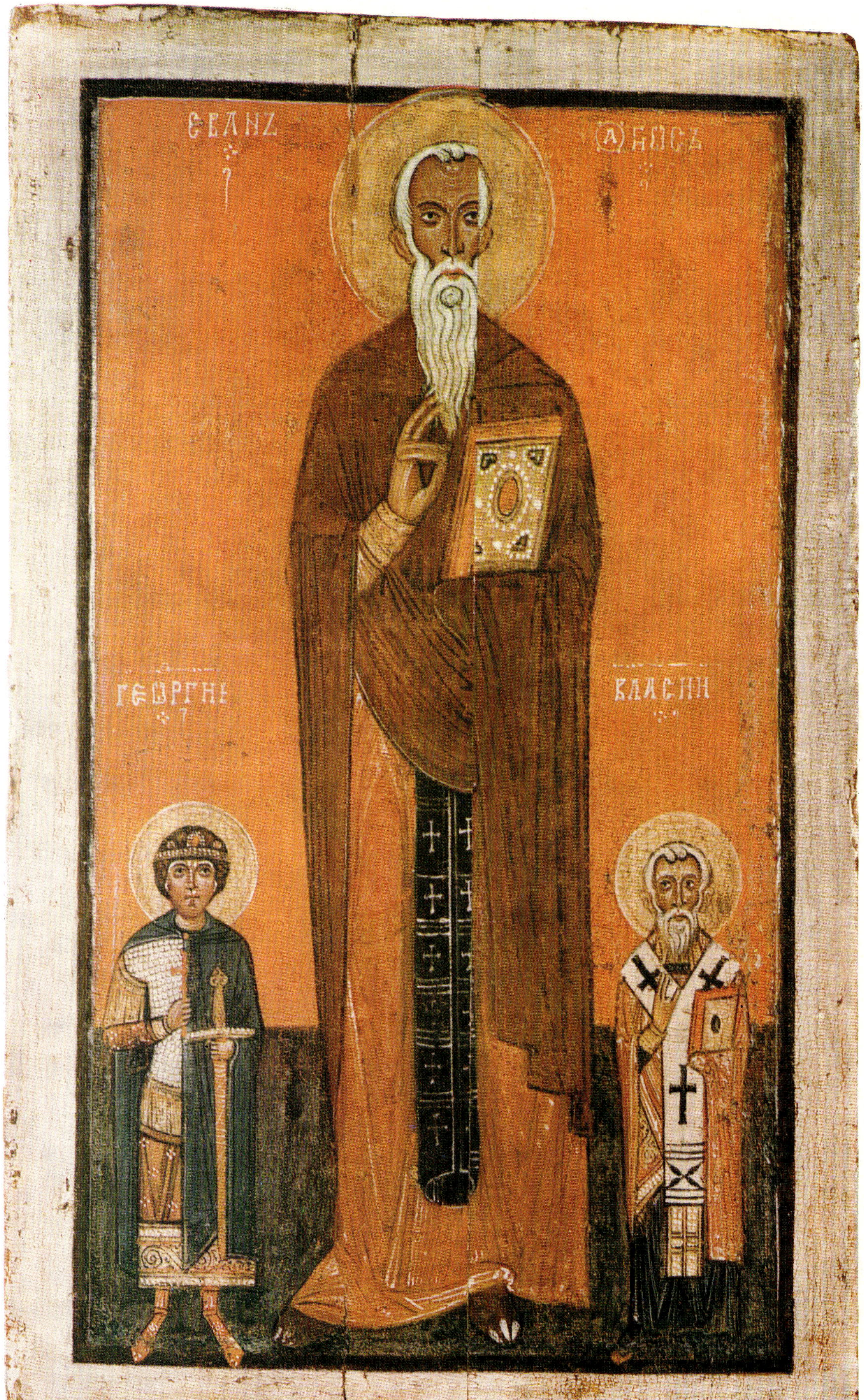

15

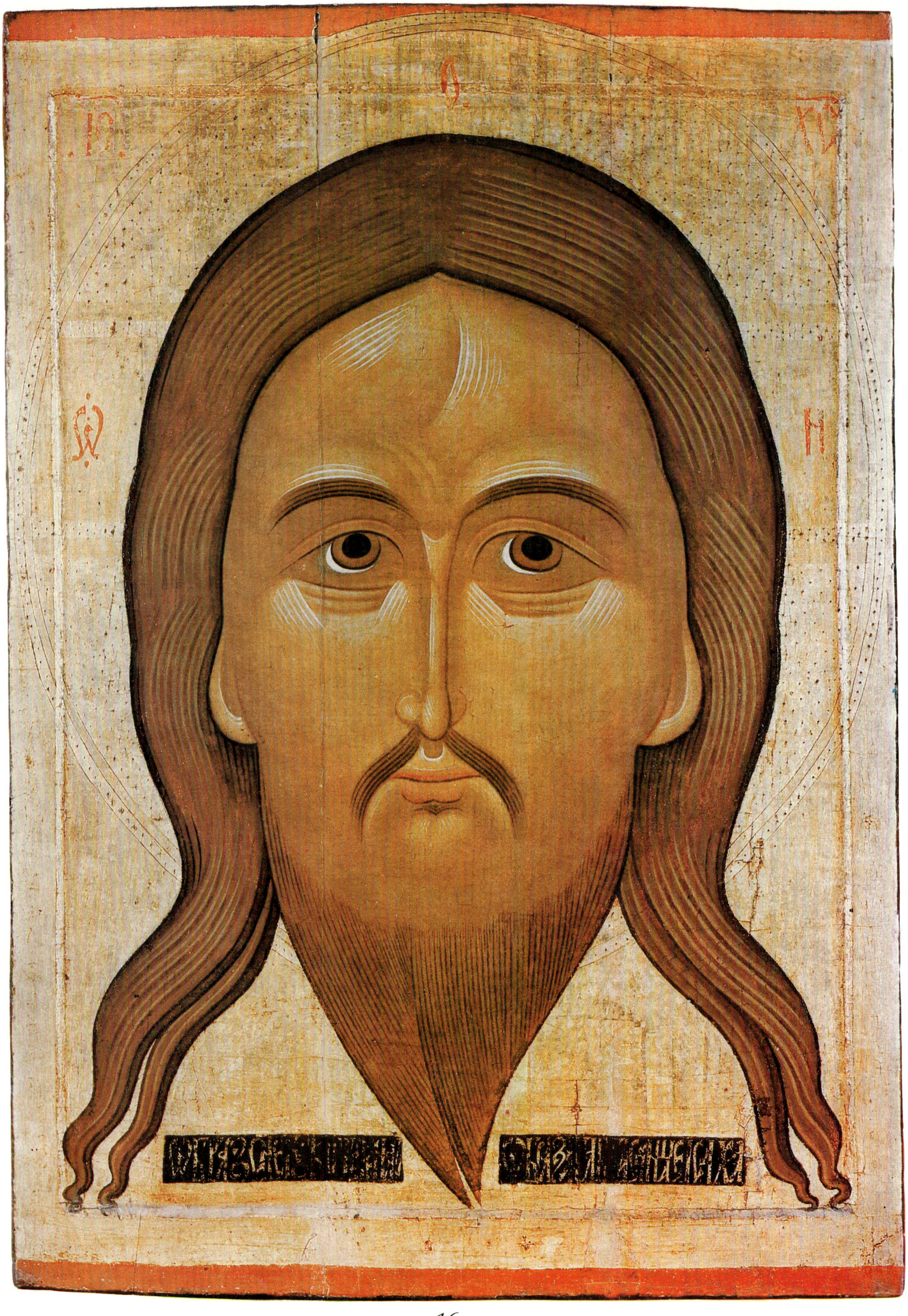

16

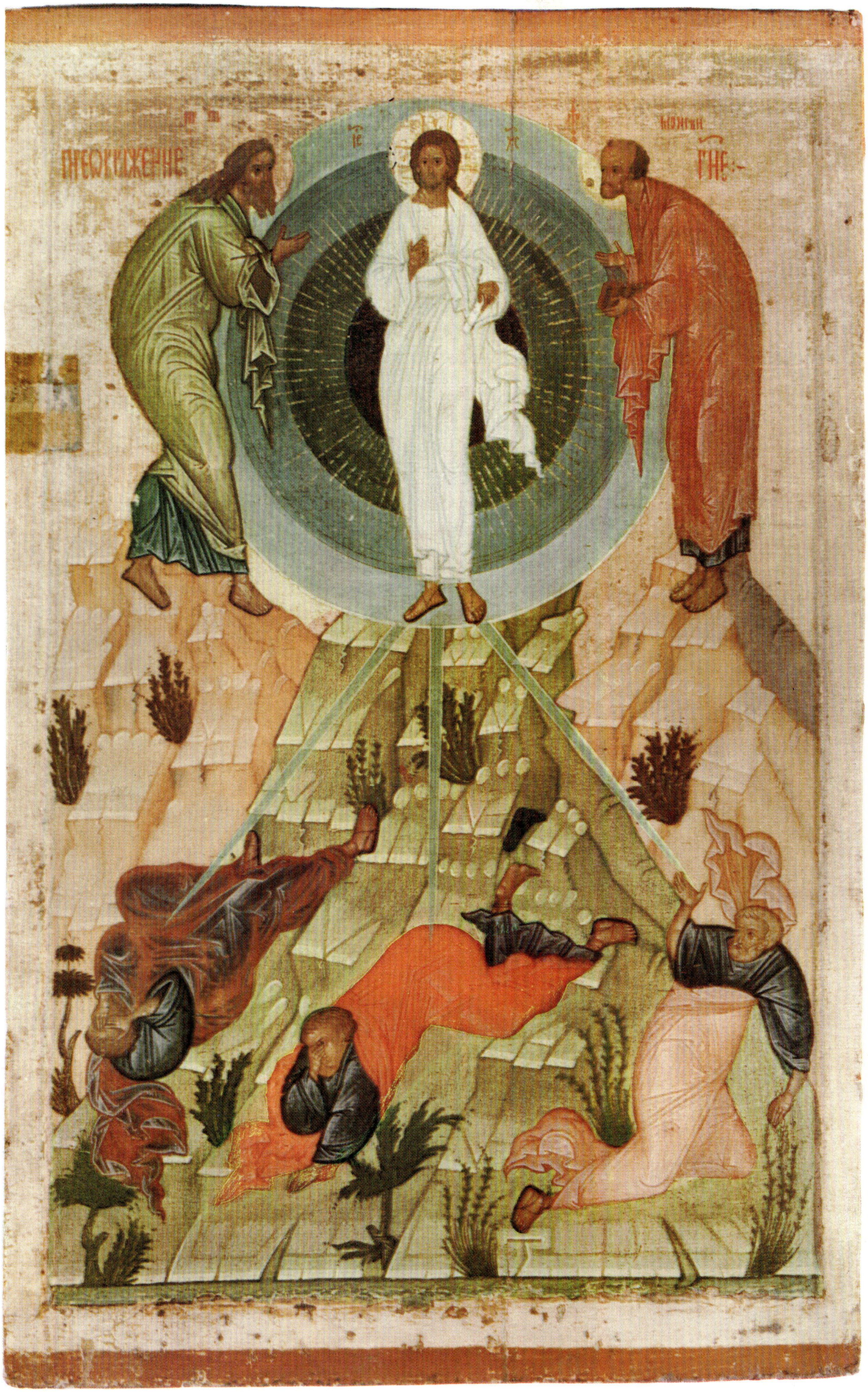

17

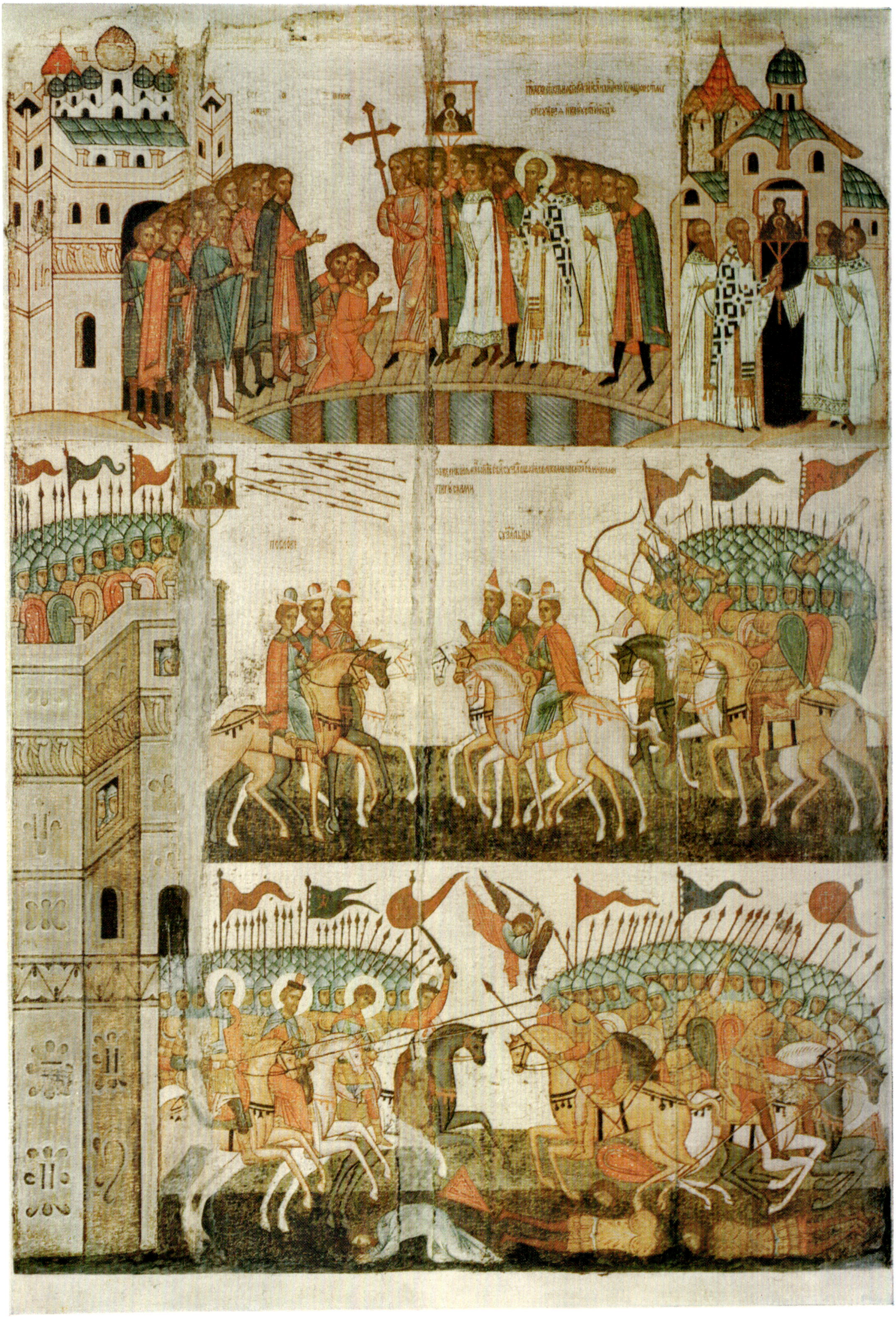

18

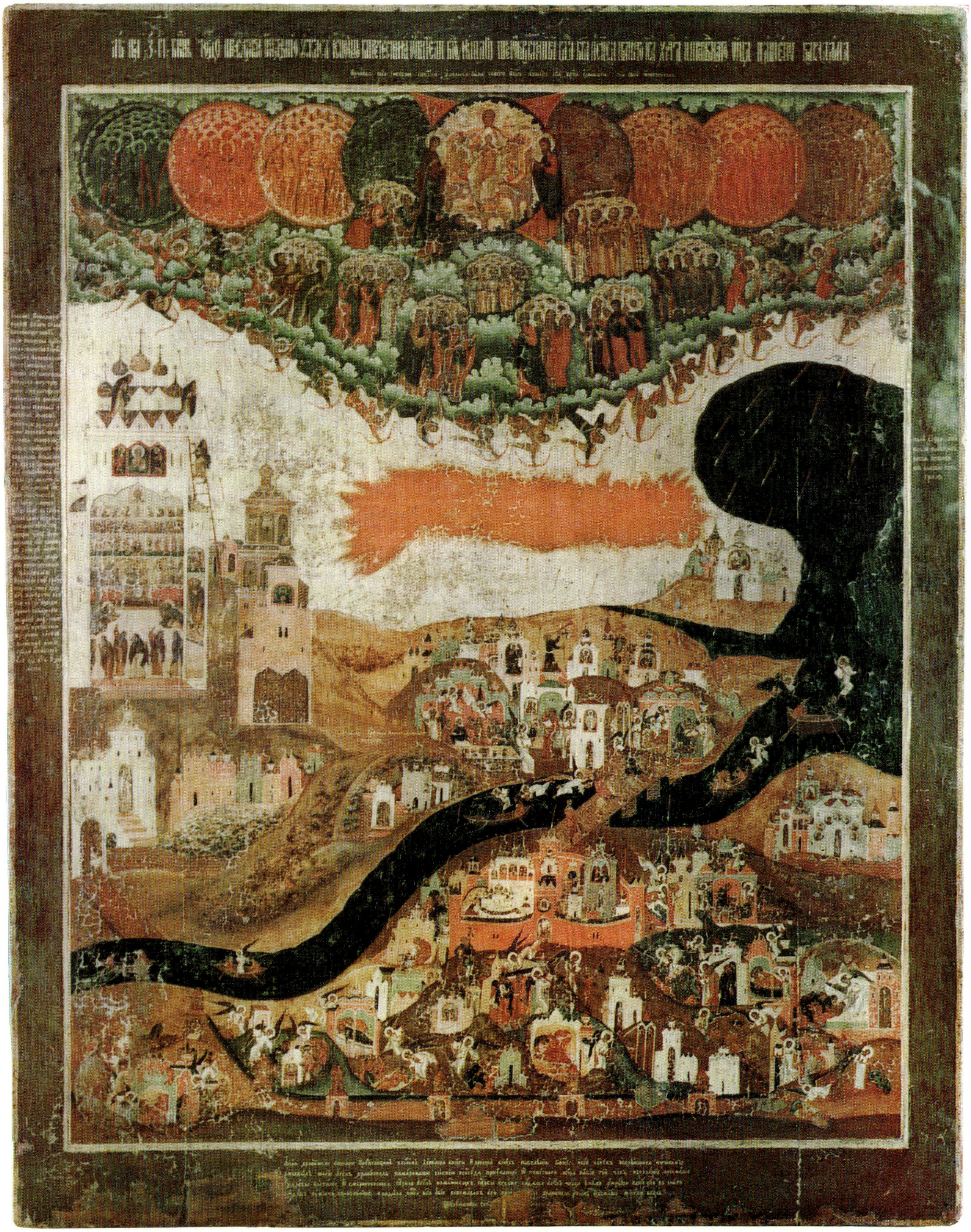

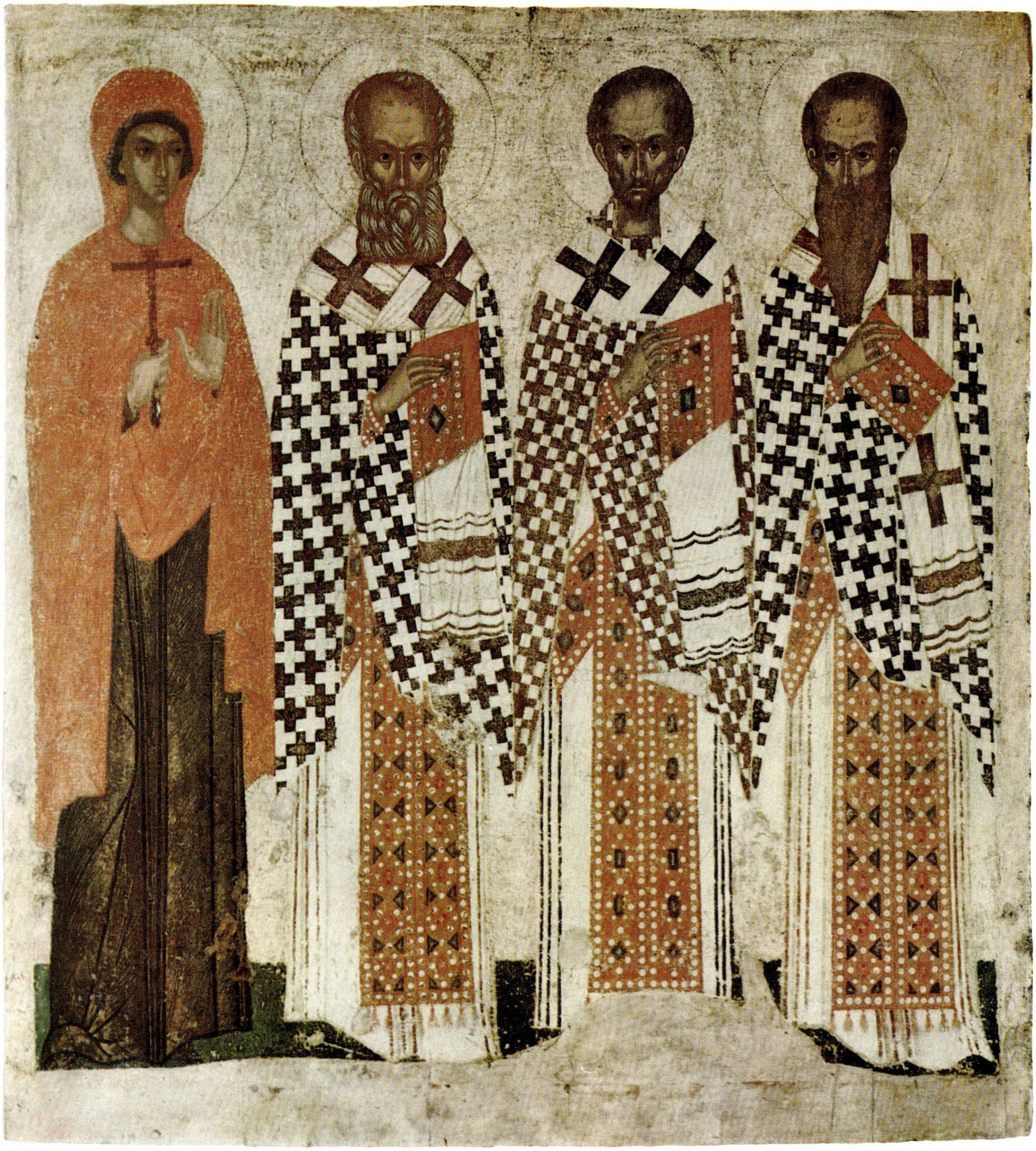

20

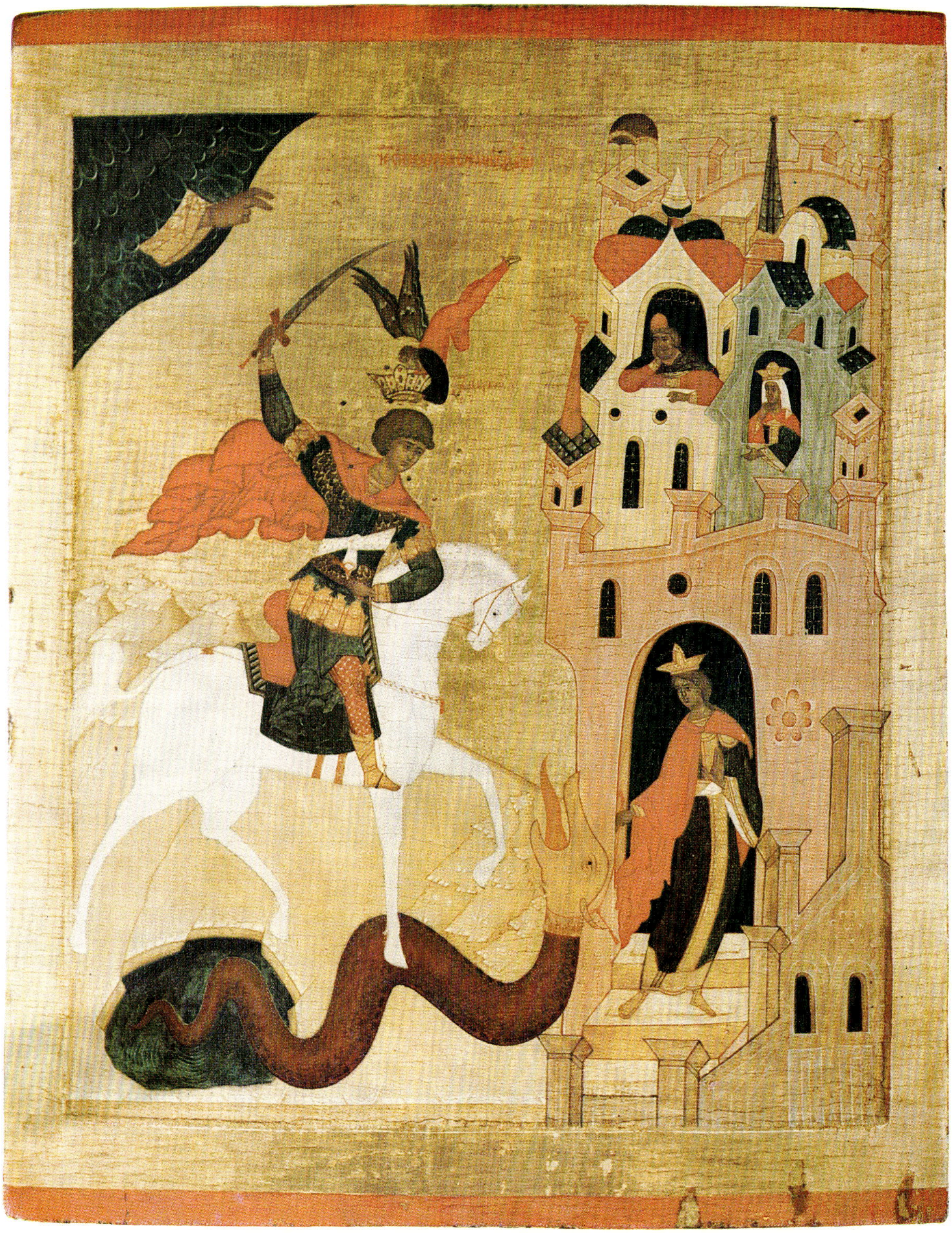

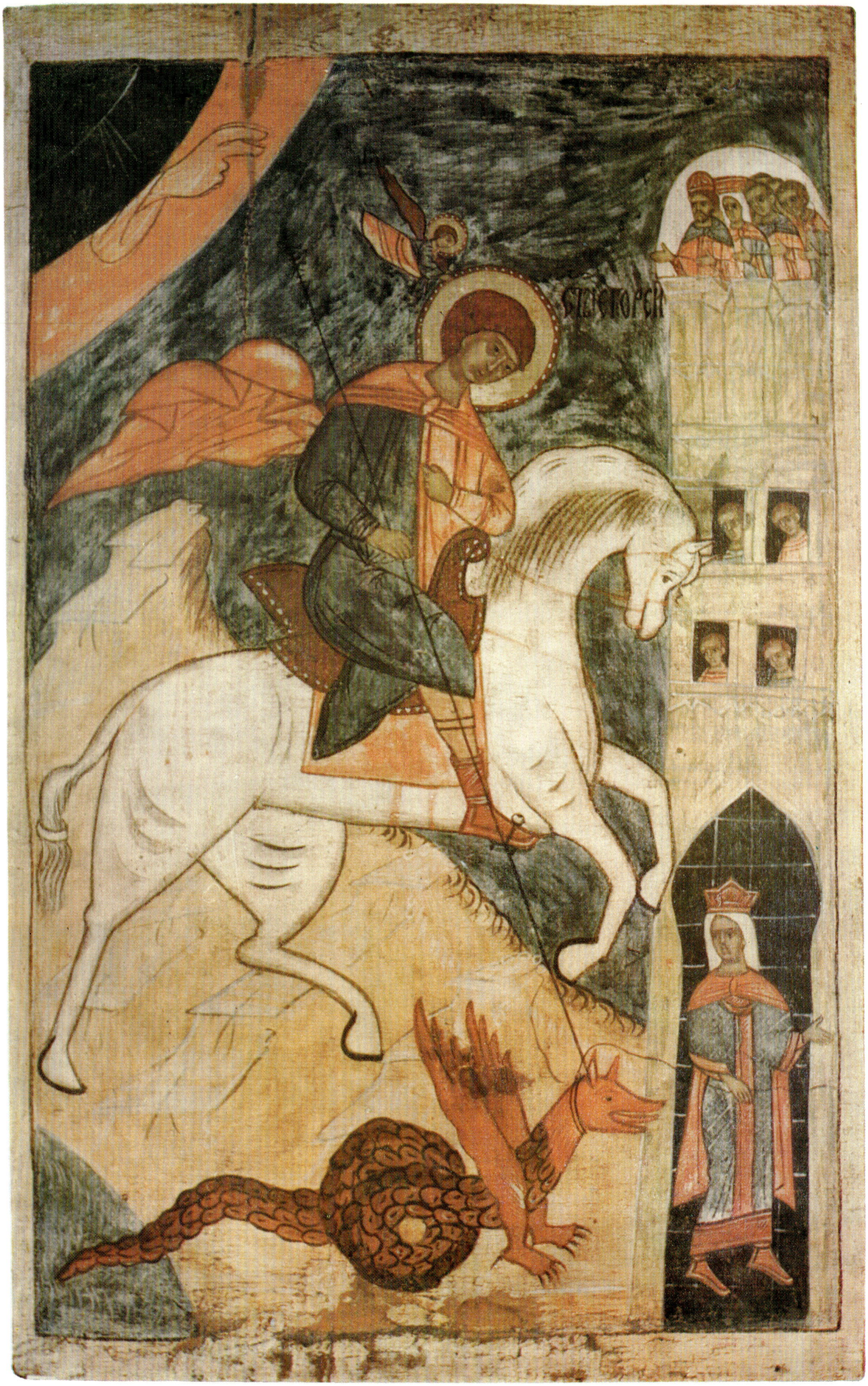

22

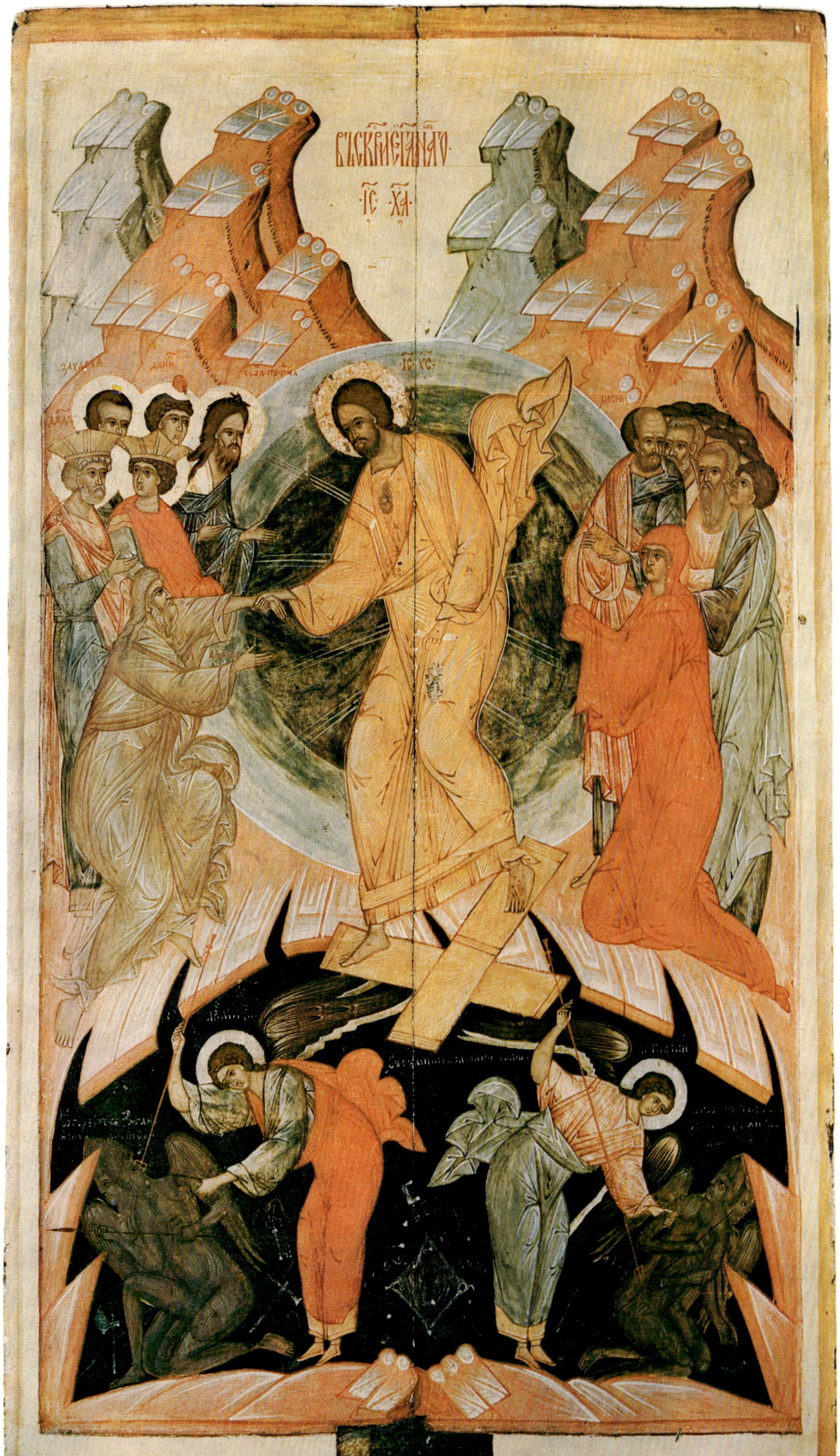

23

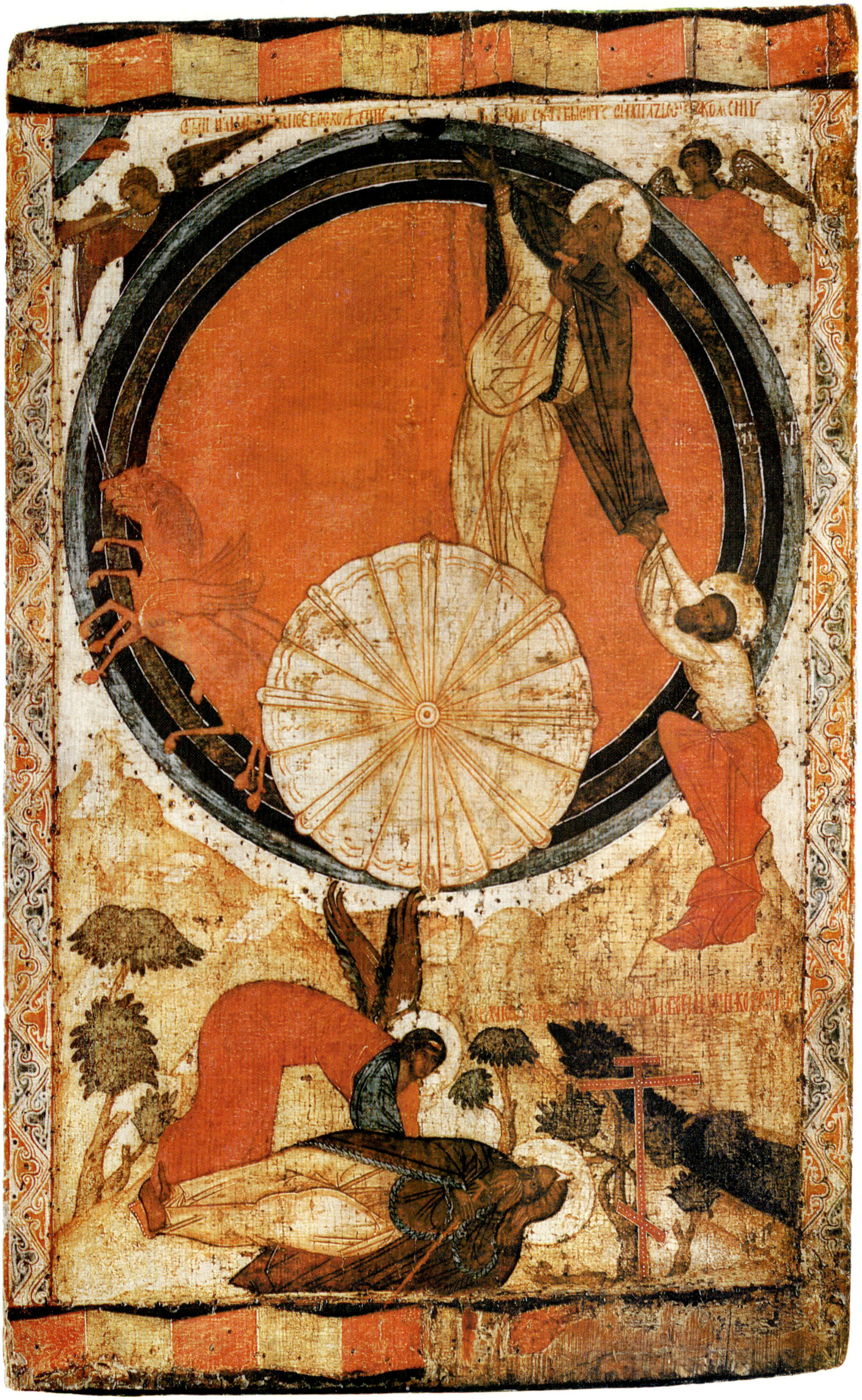

24

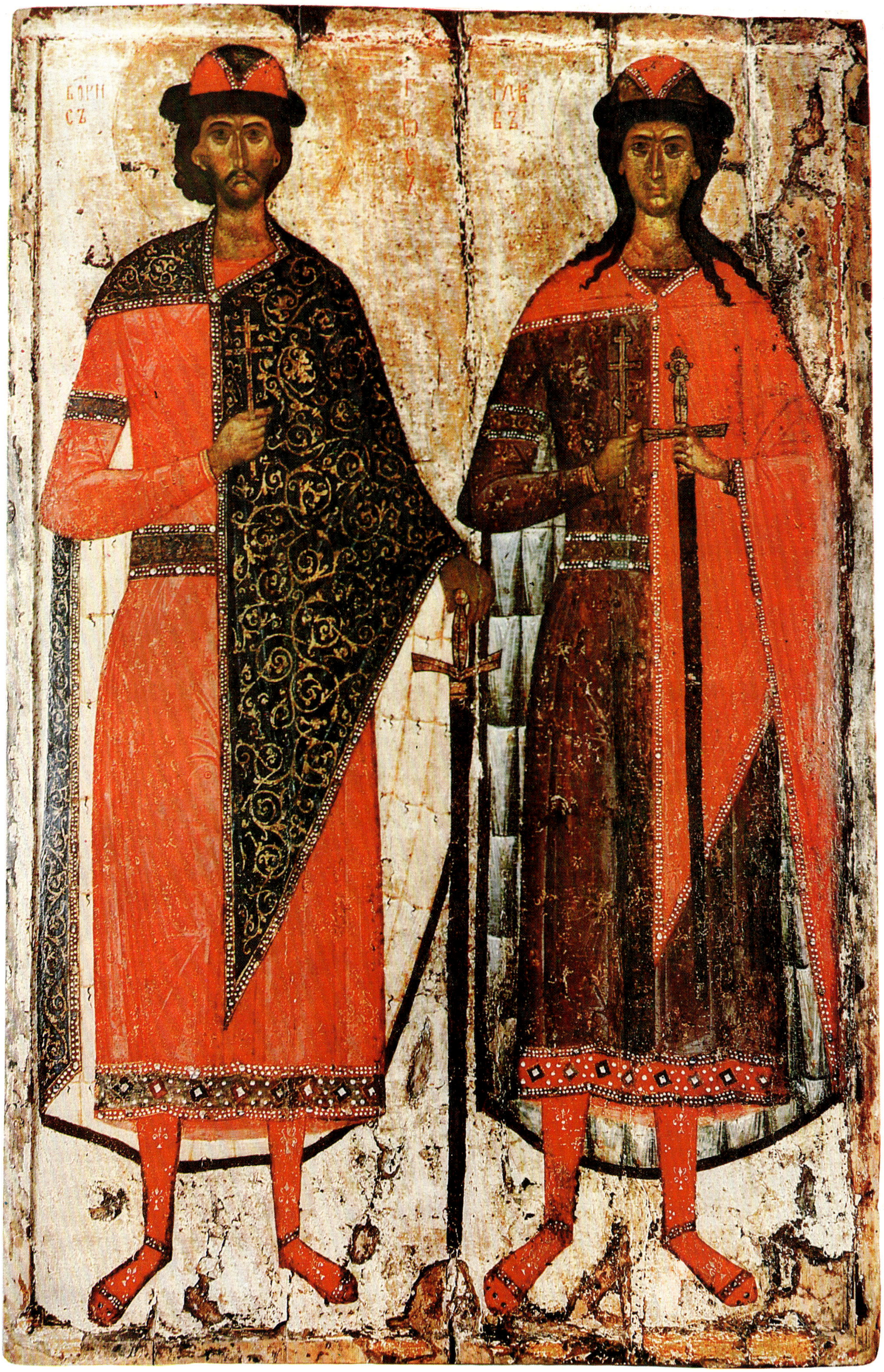

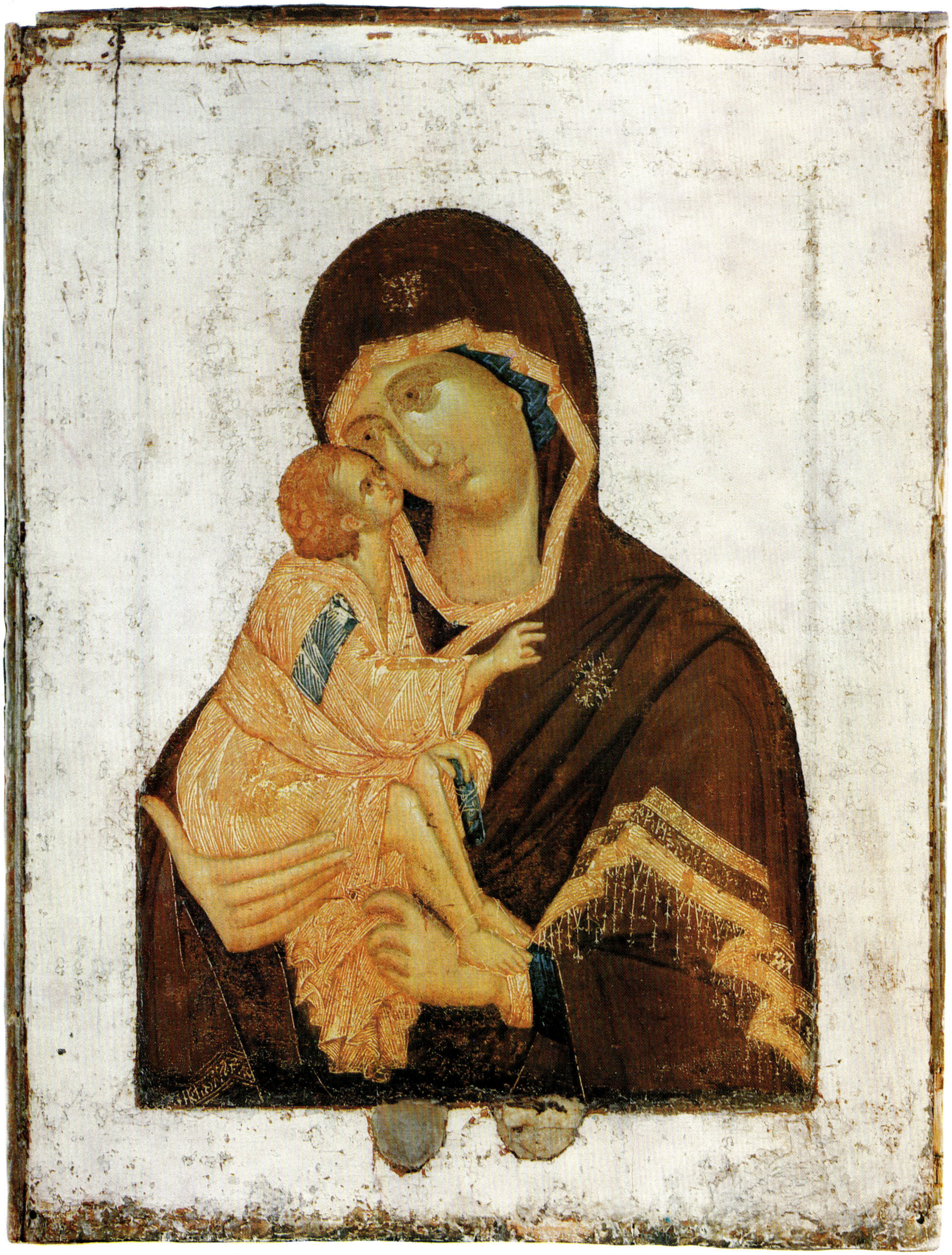

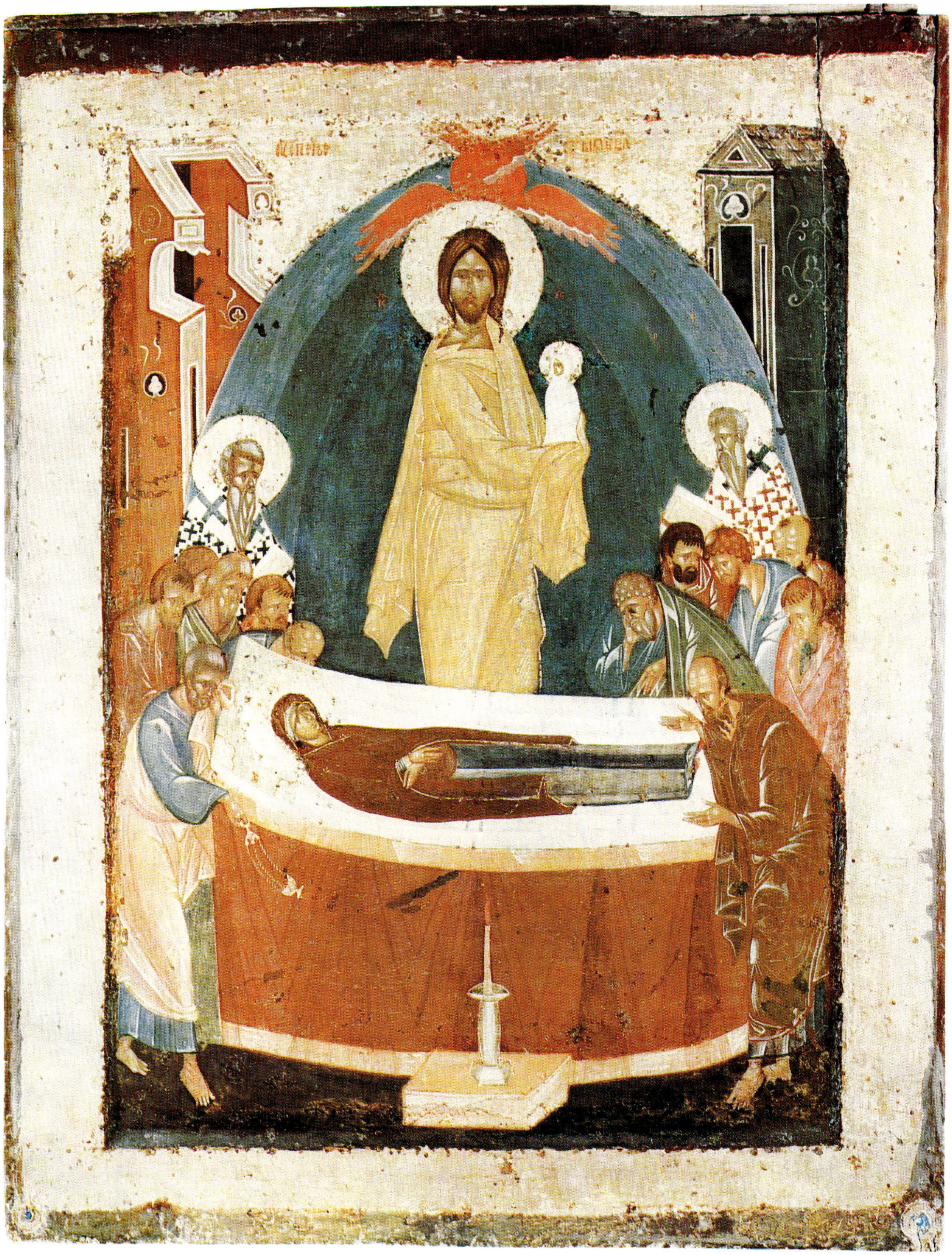

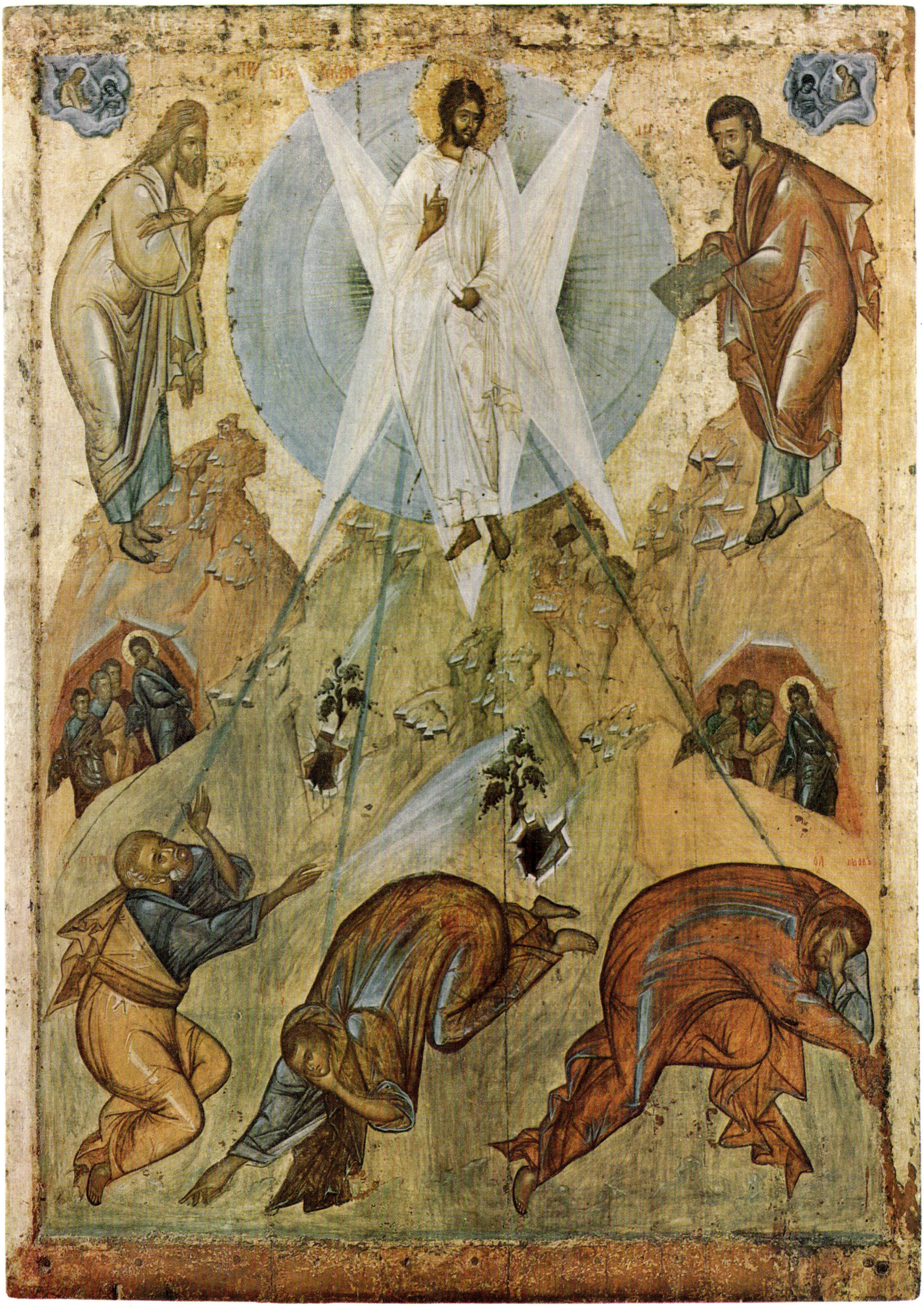

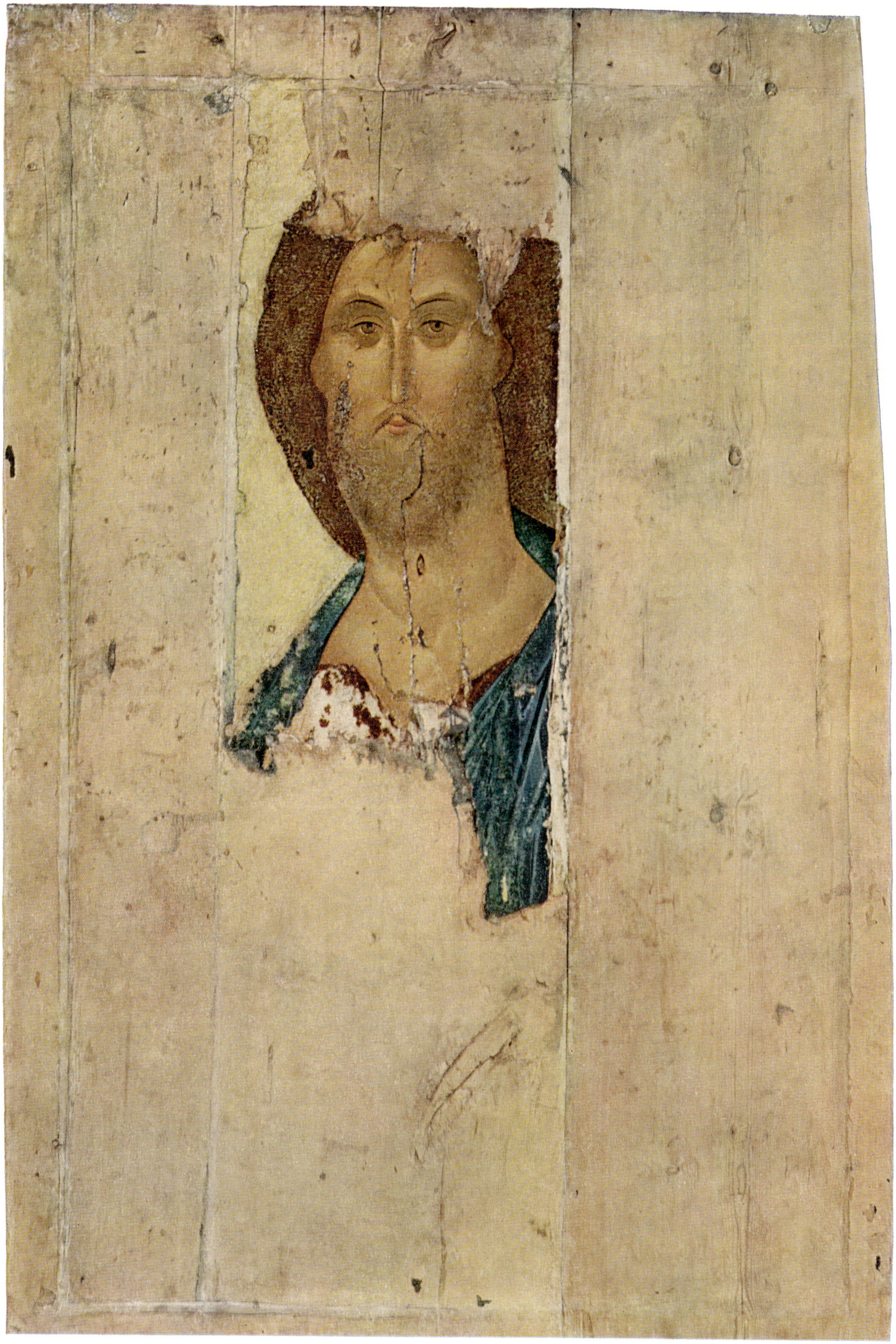

29

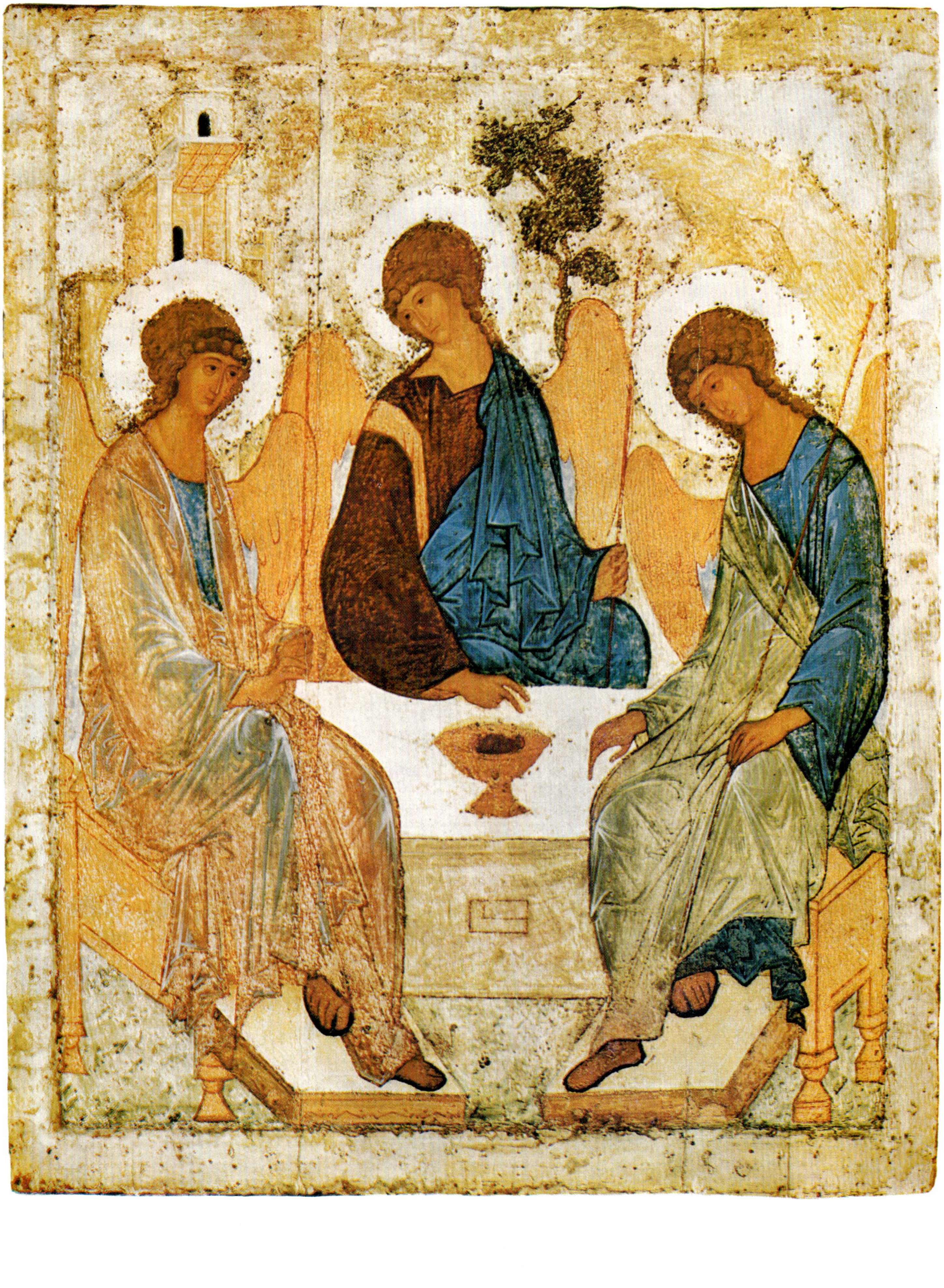

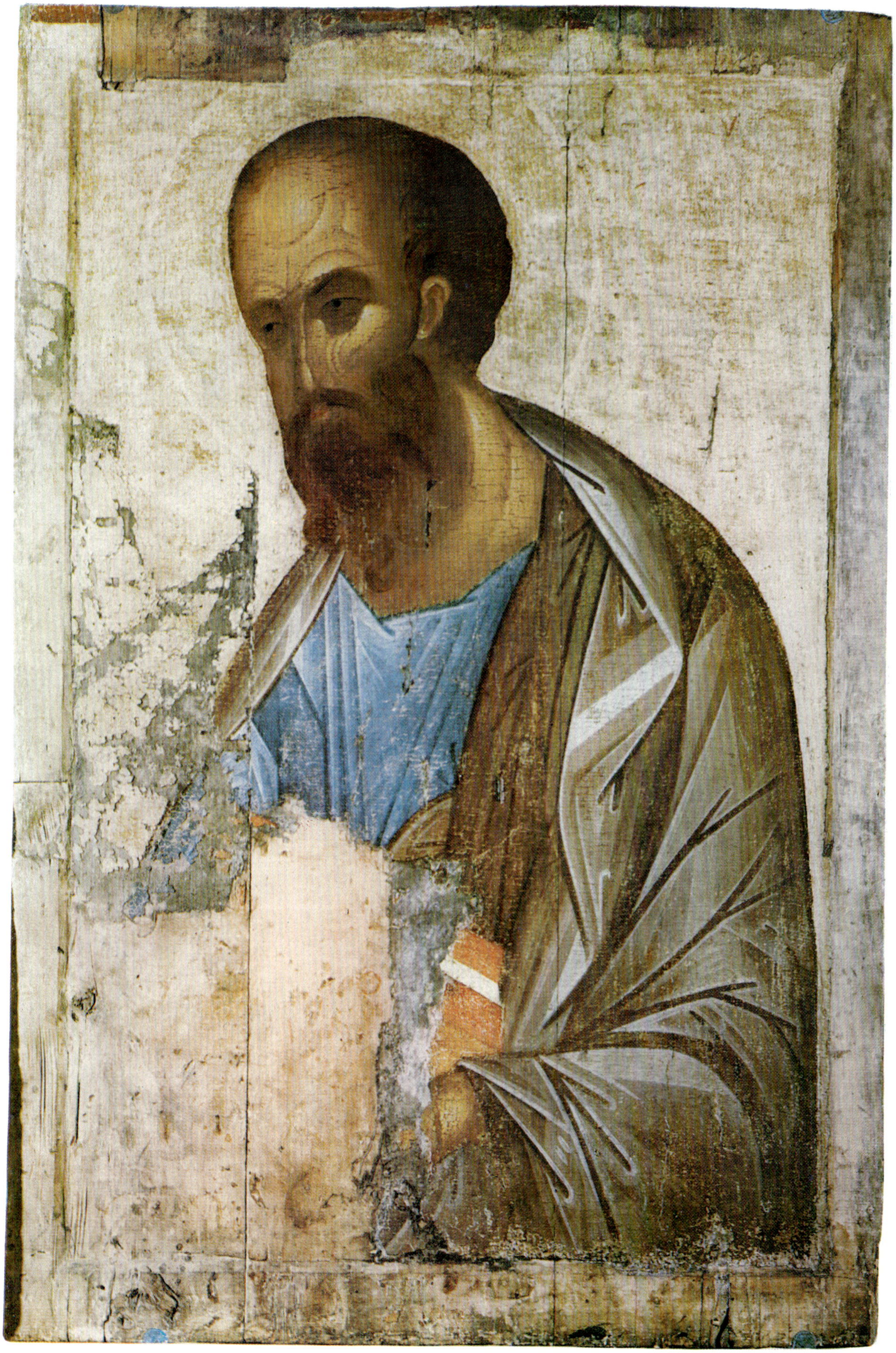

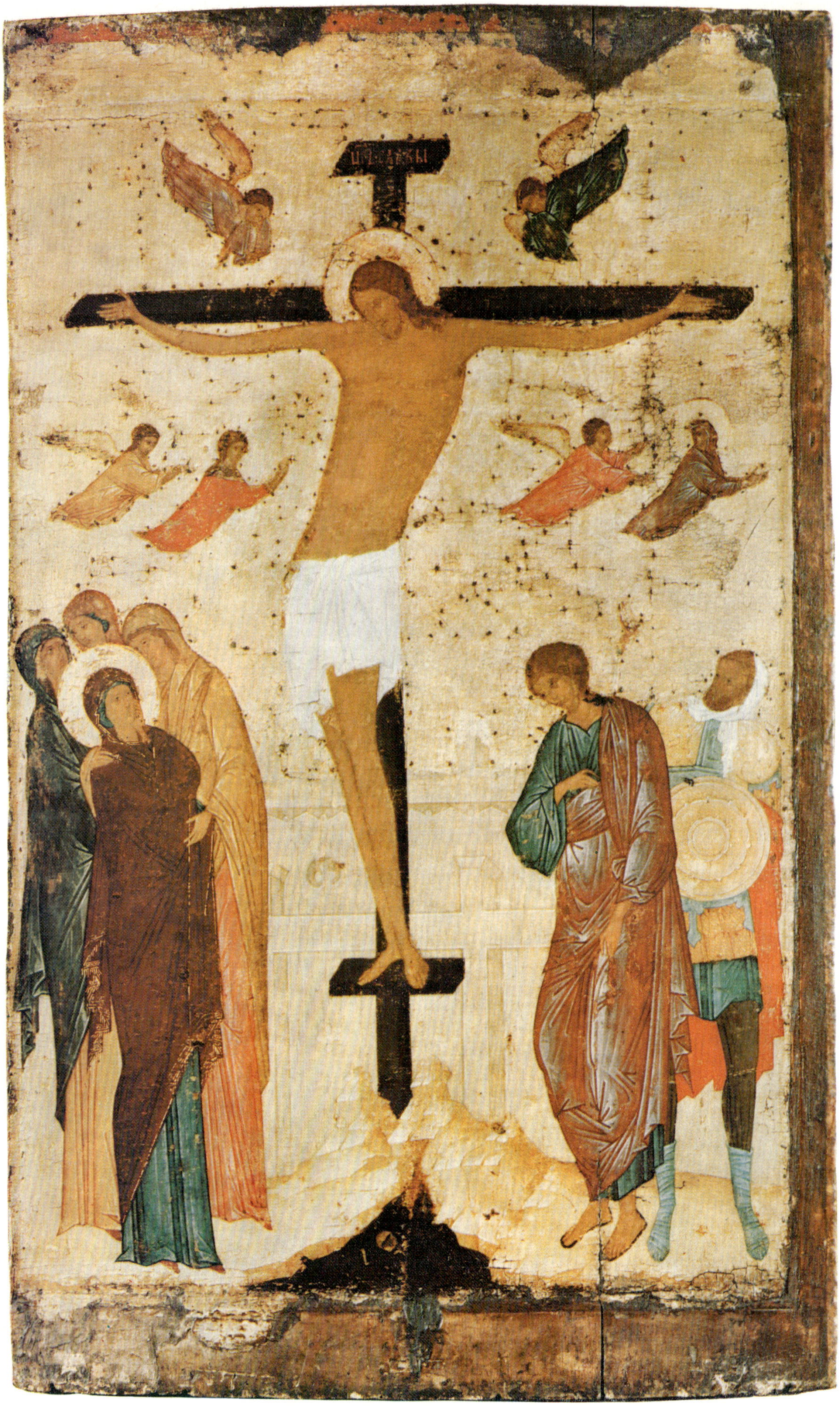

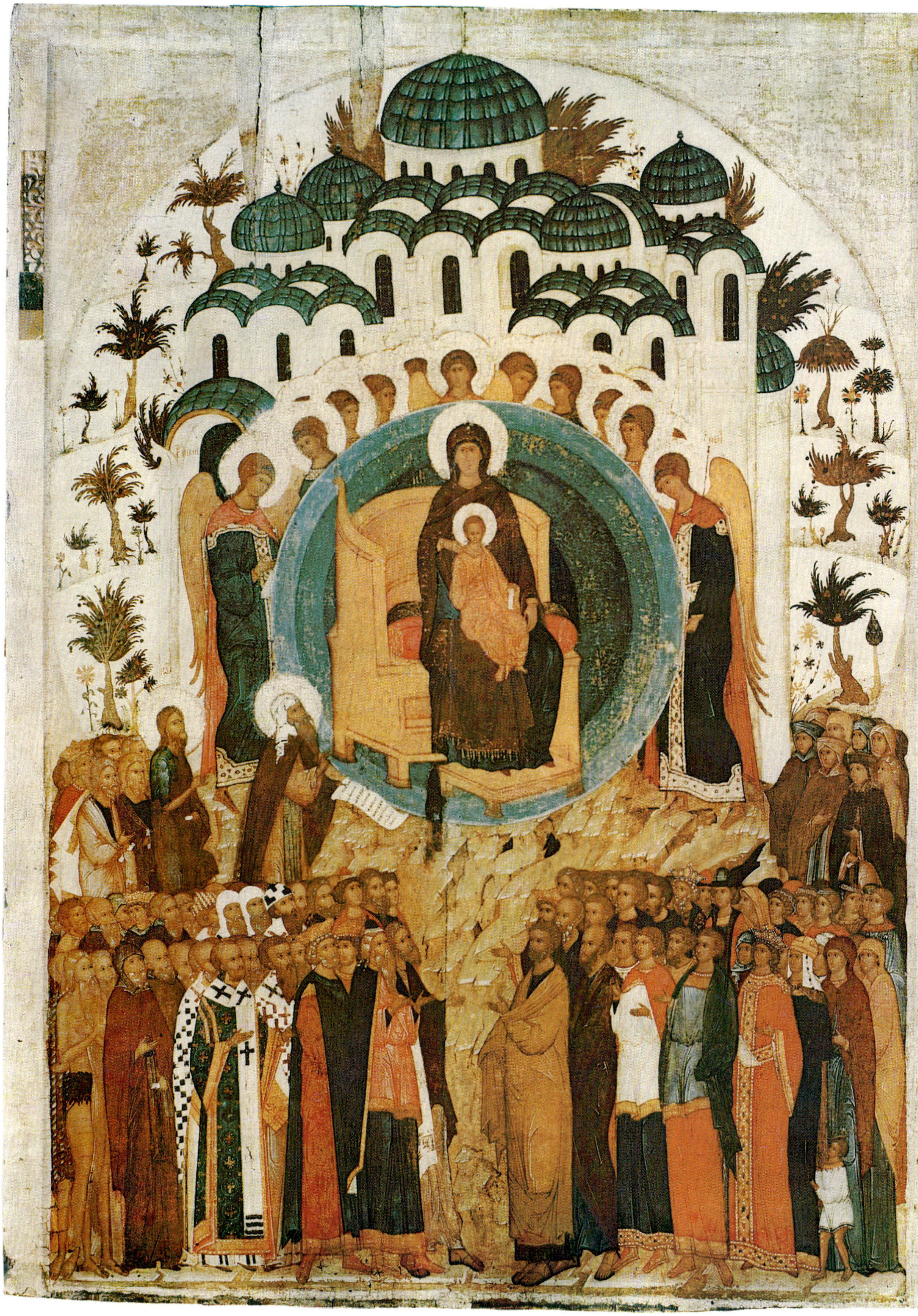

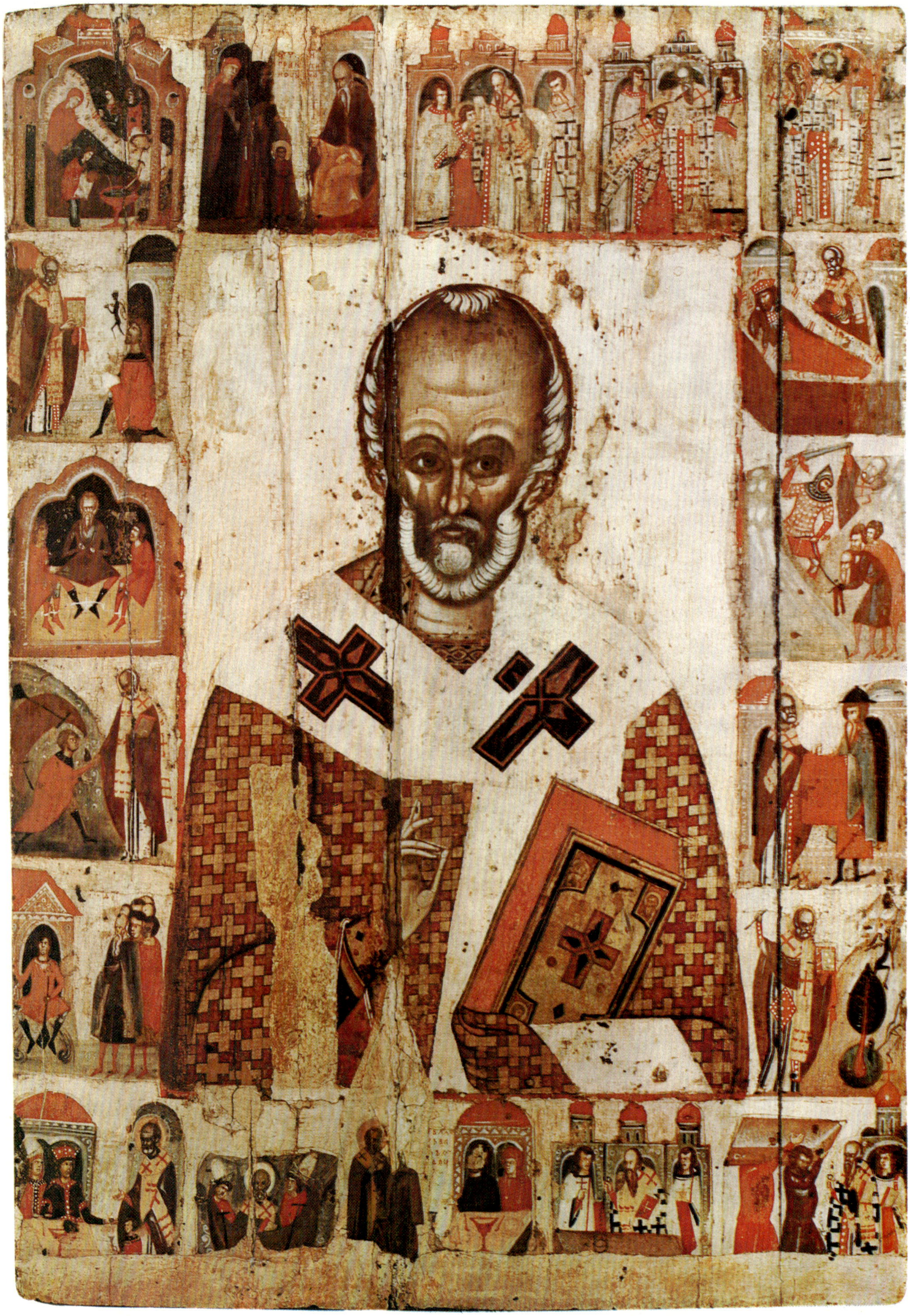

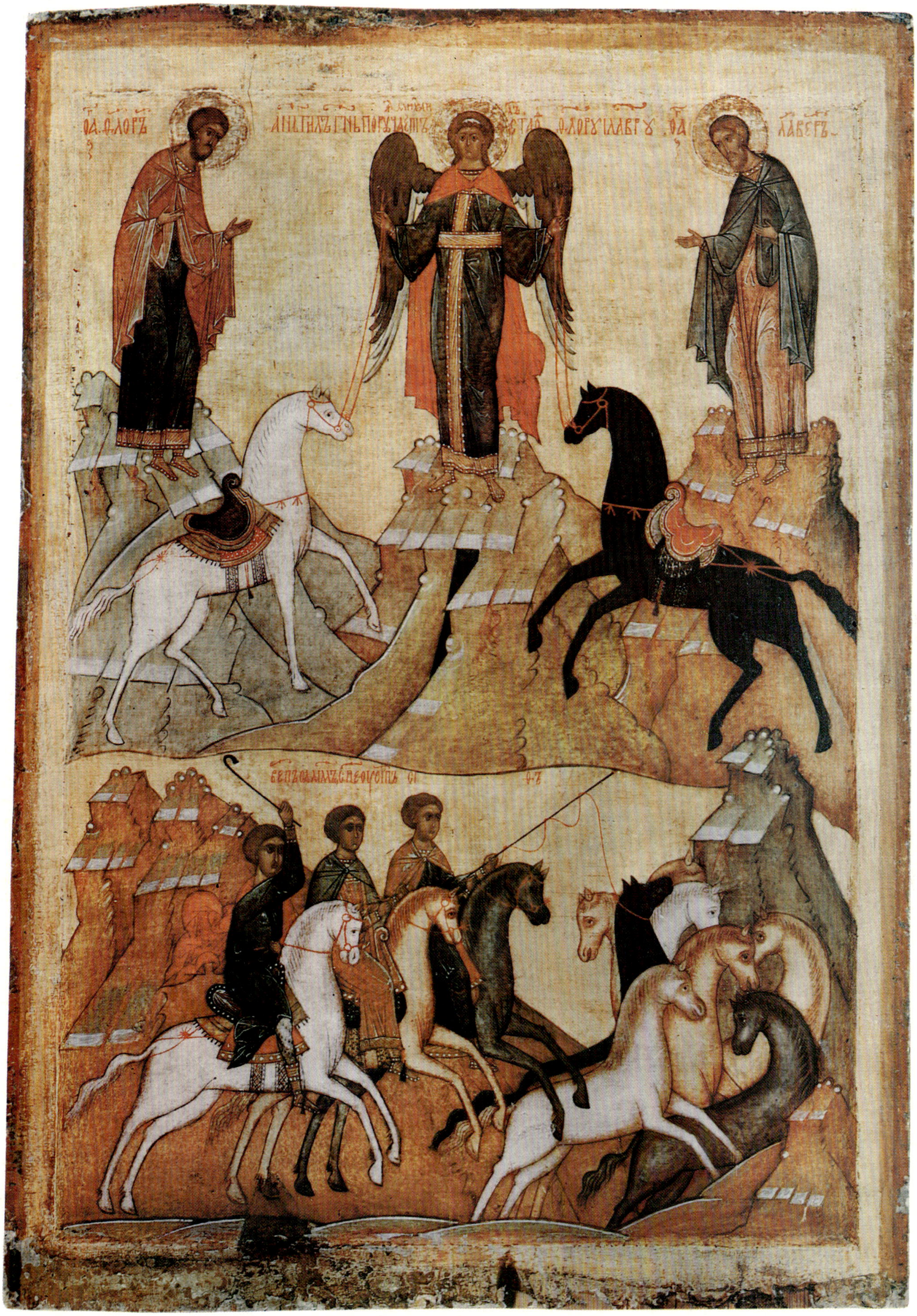

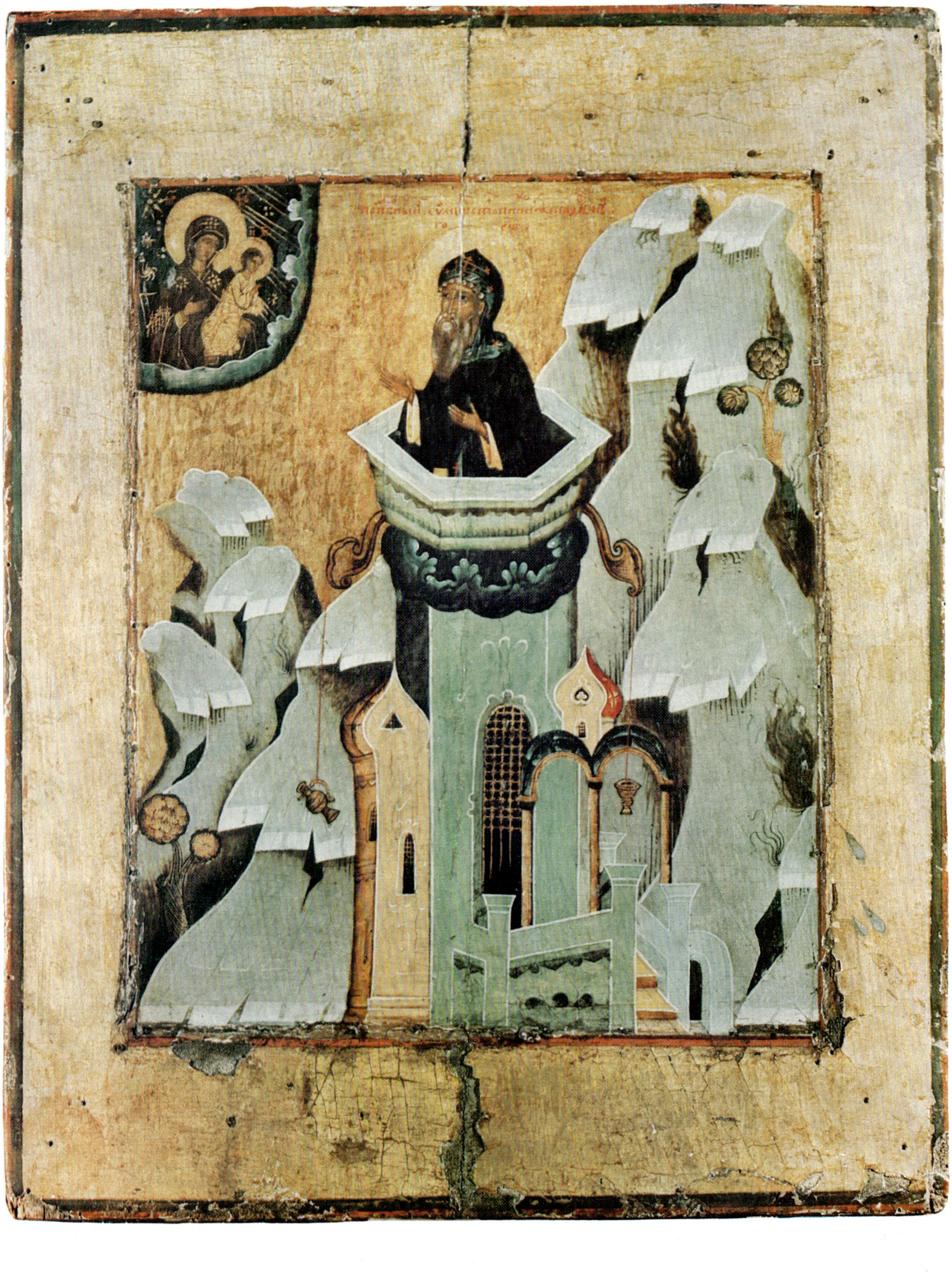

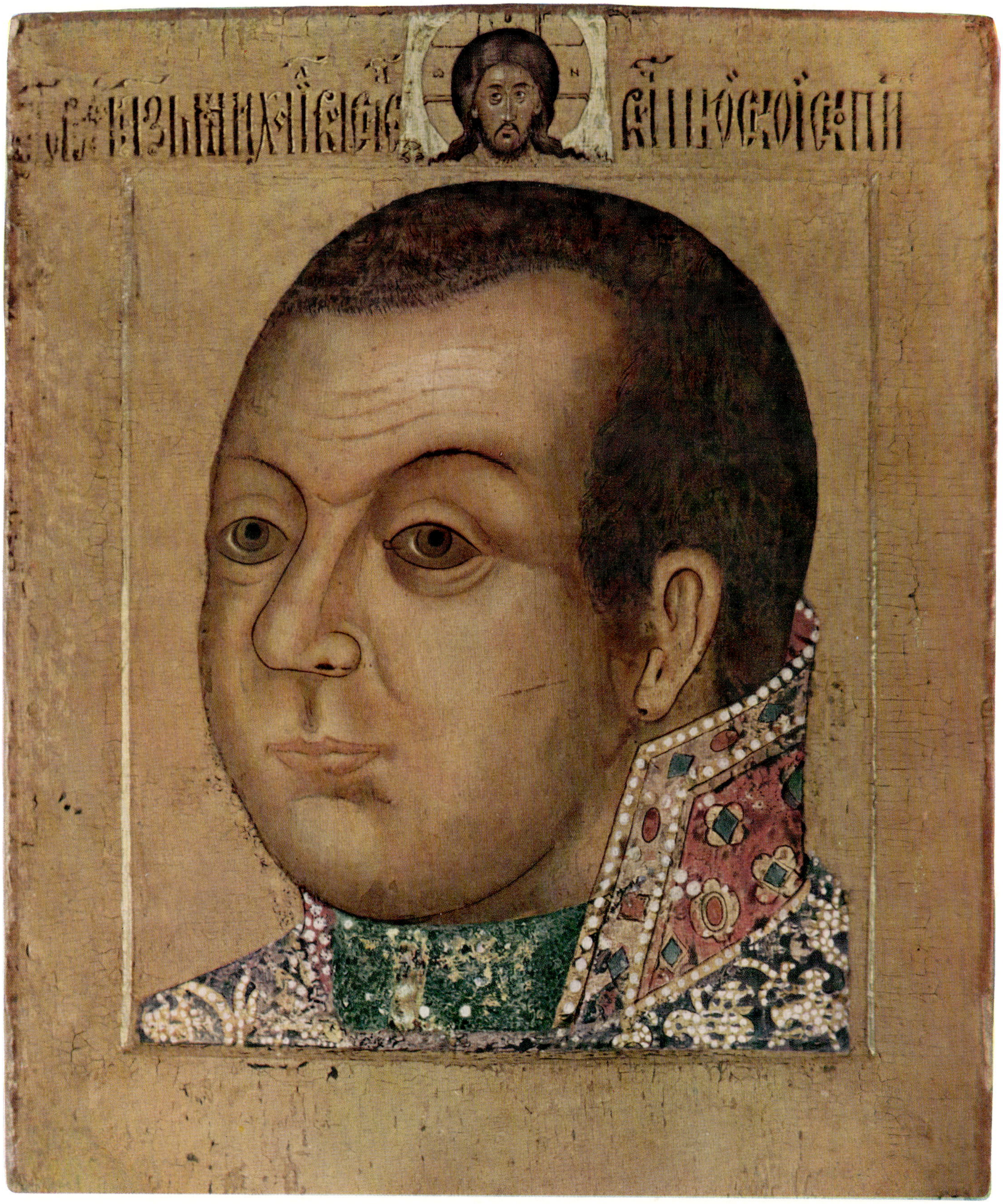

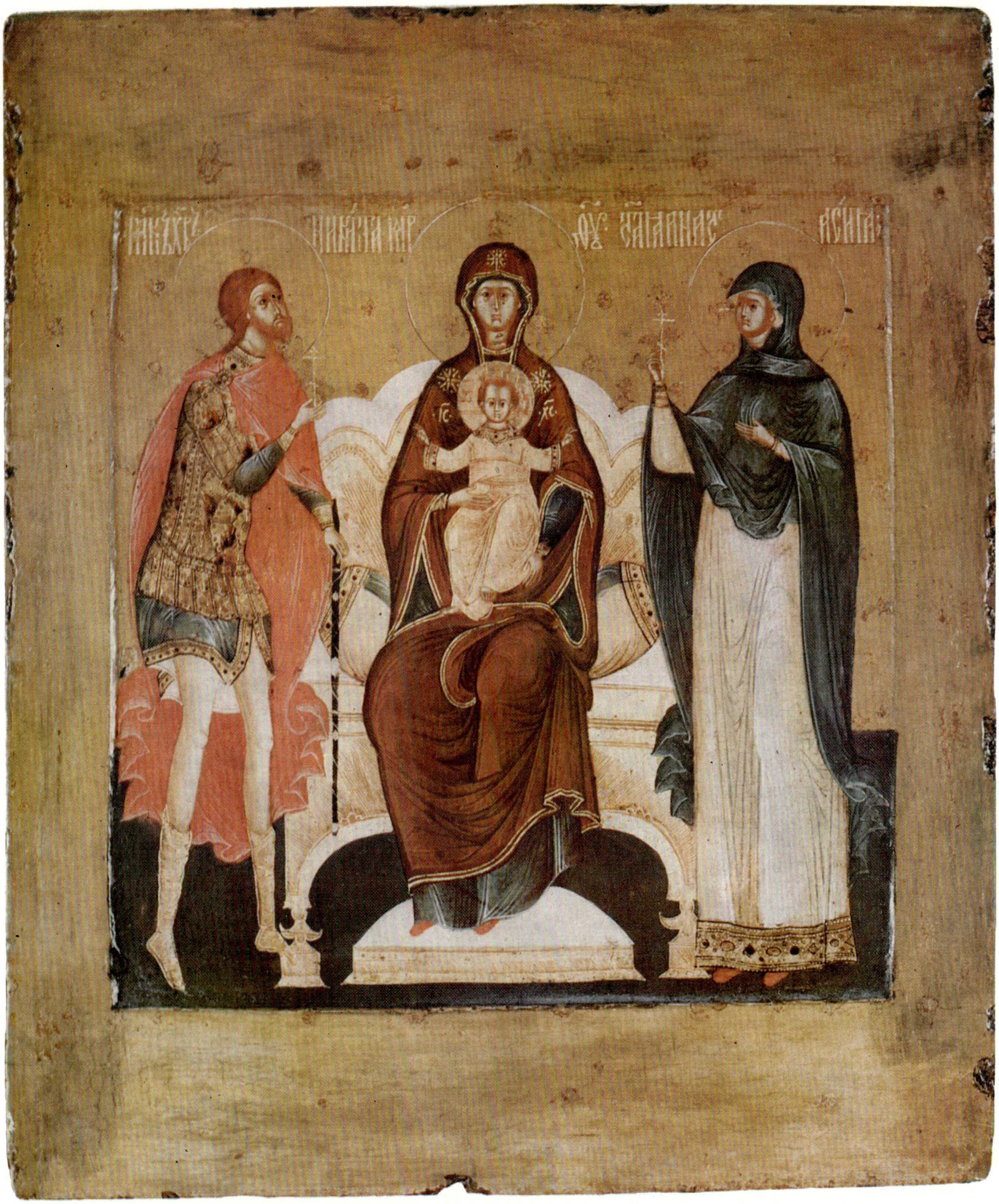

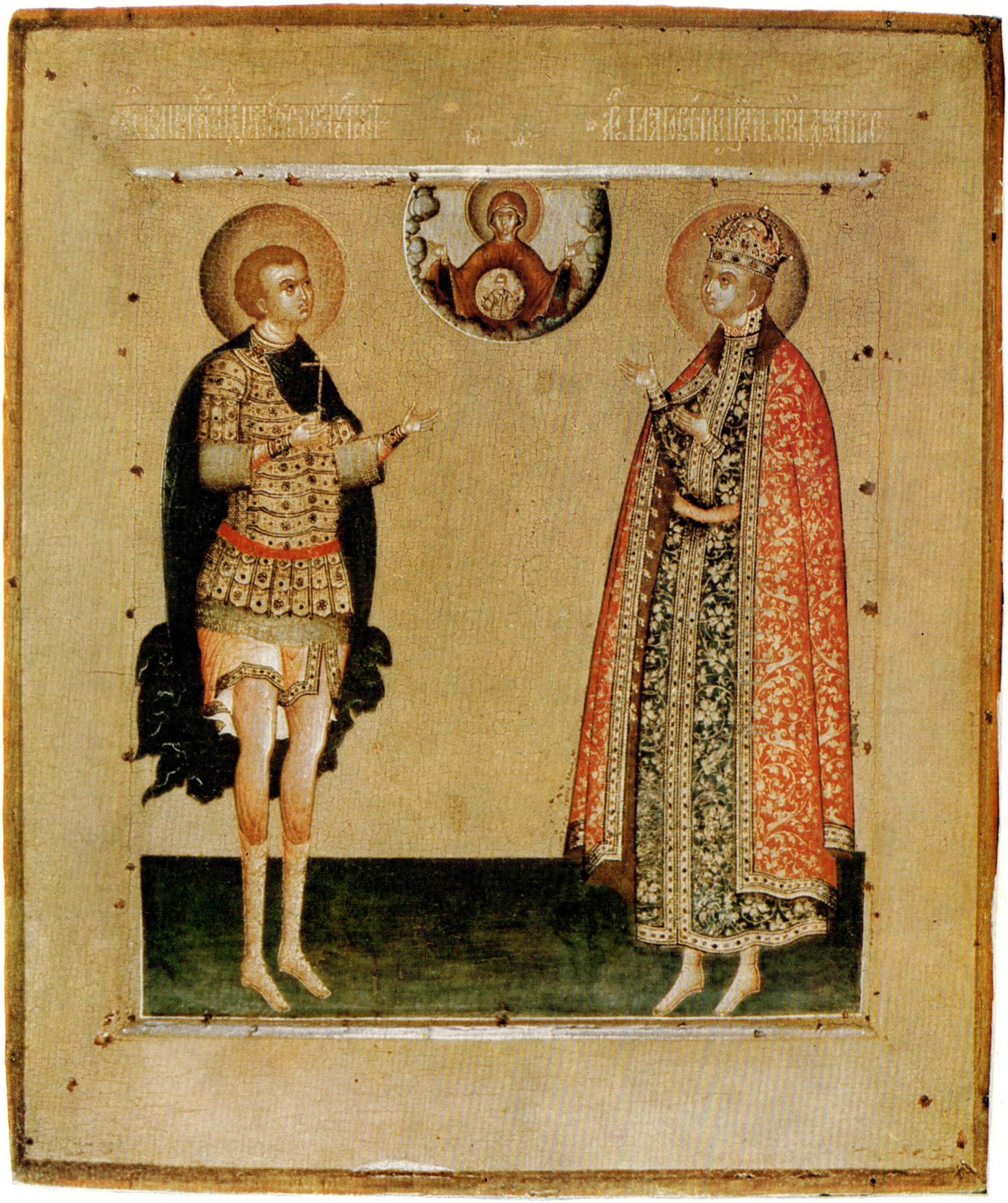

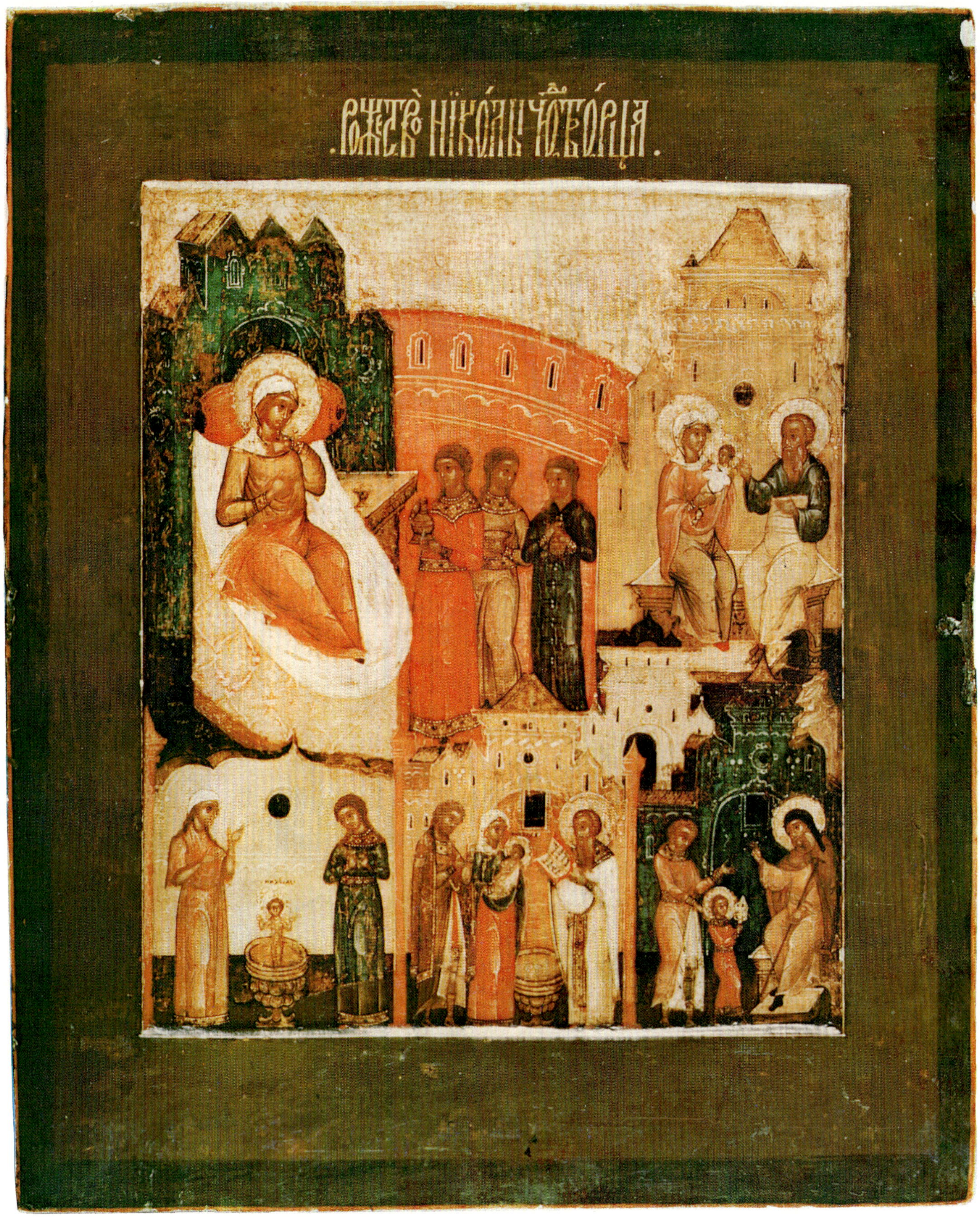

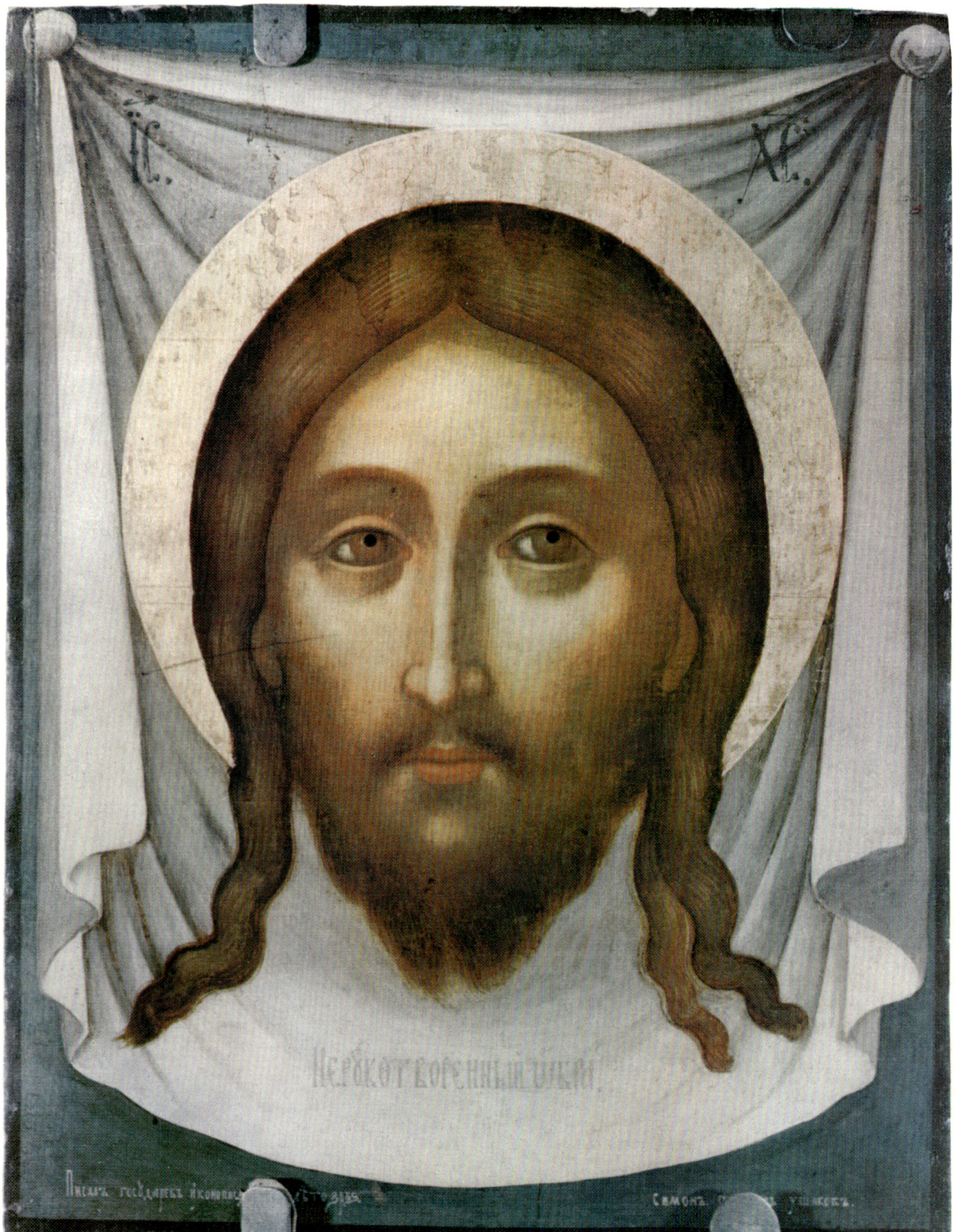
ІС
ХС

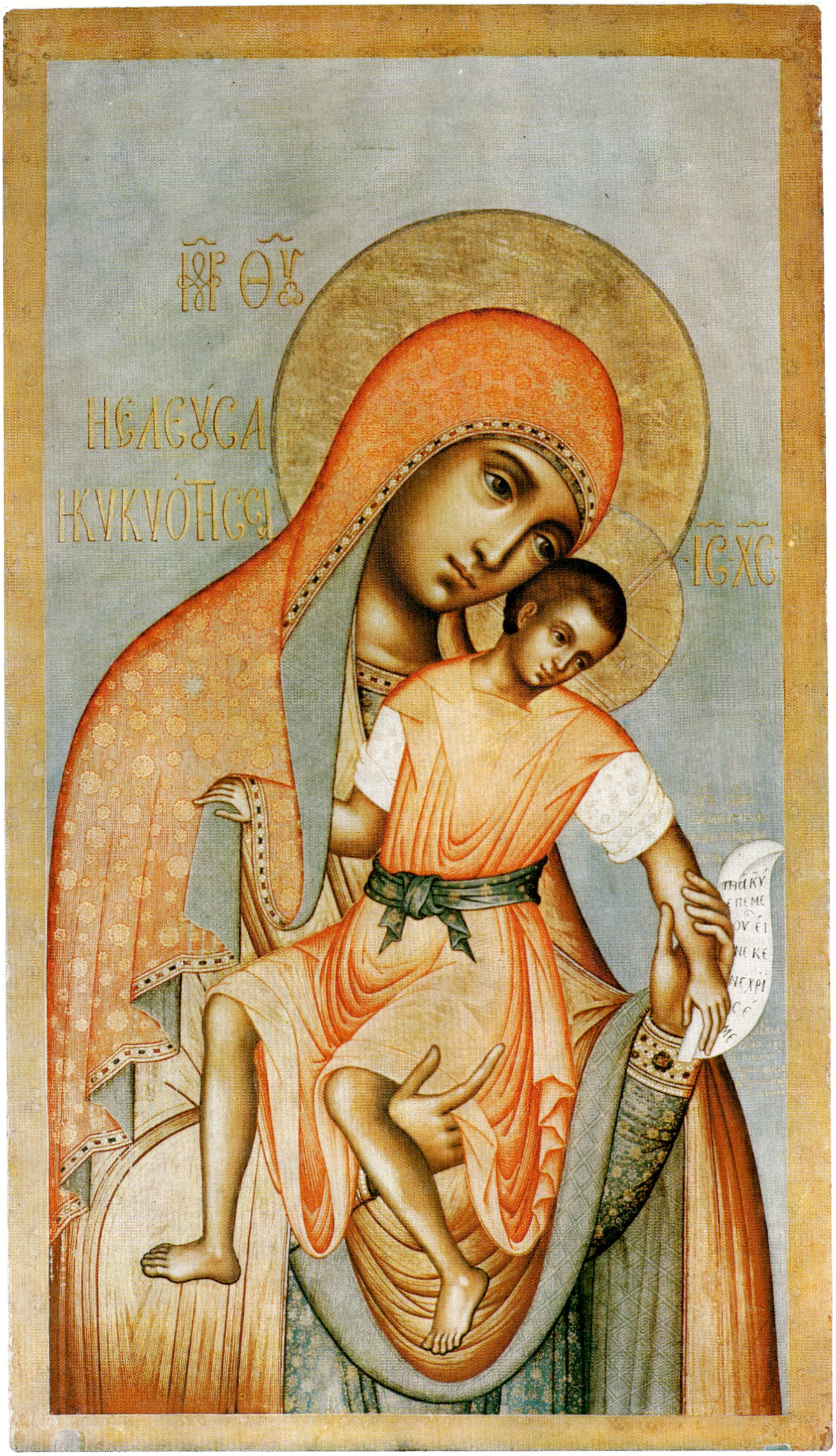
ΜΡ ΘΥ
Η ΕΛΕΟΥΣΑ
Η ΚΥΚΚΩΤΗΣΣΑ
IC XC

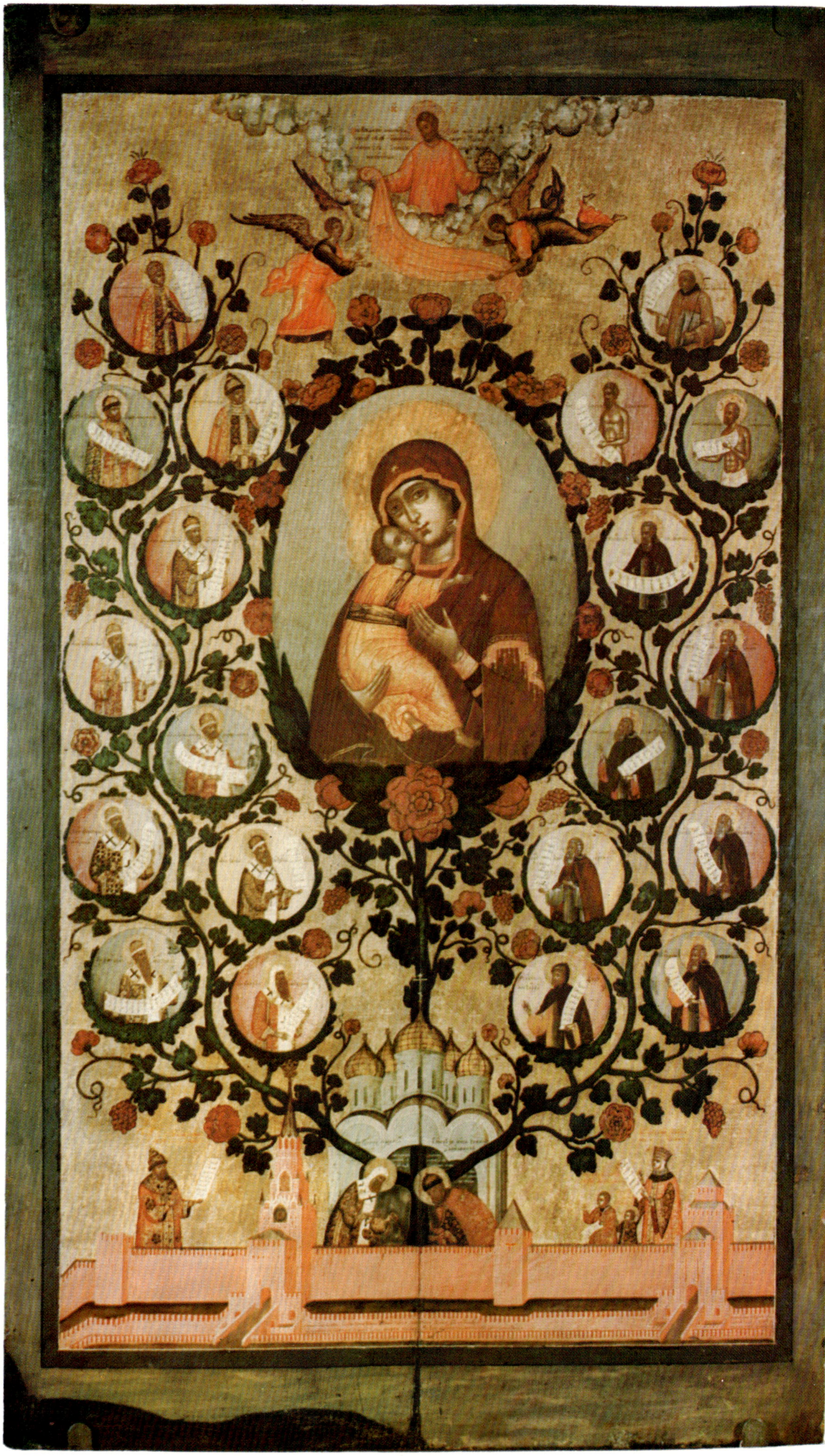

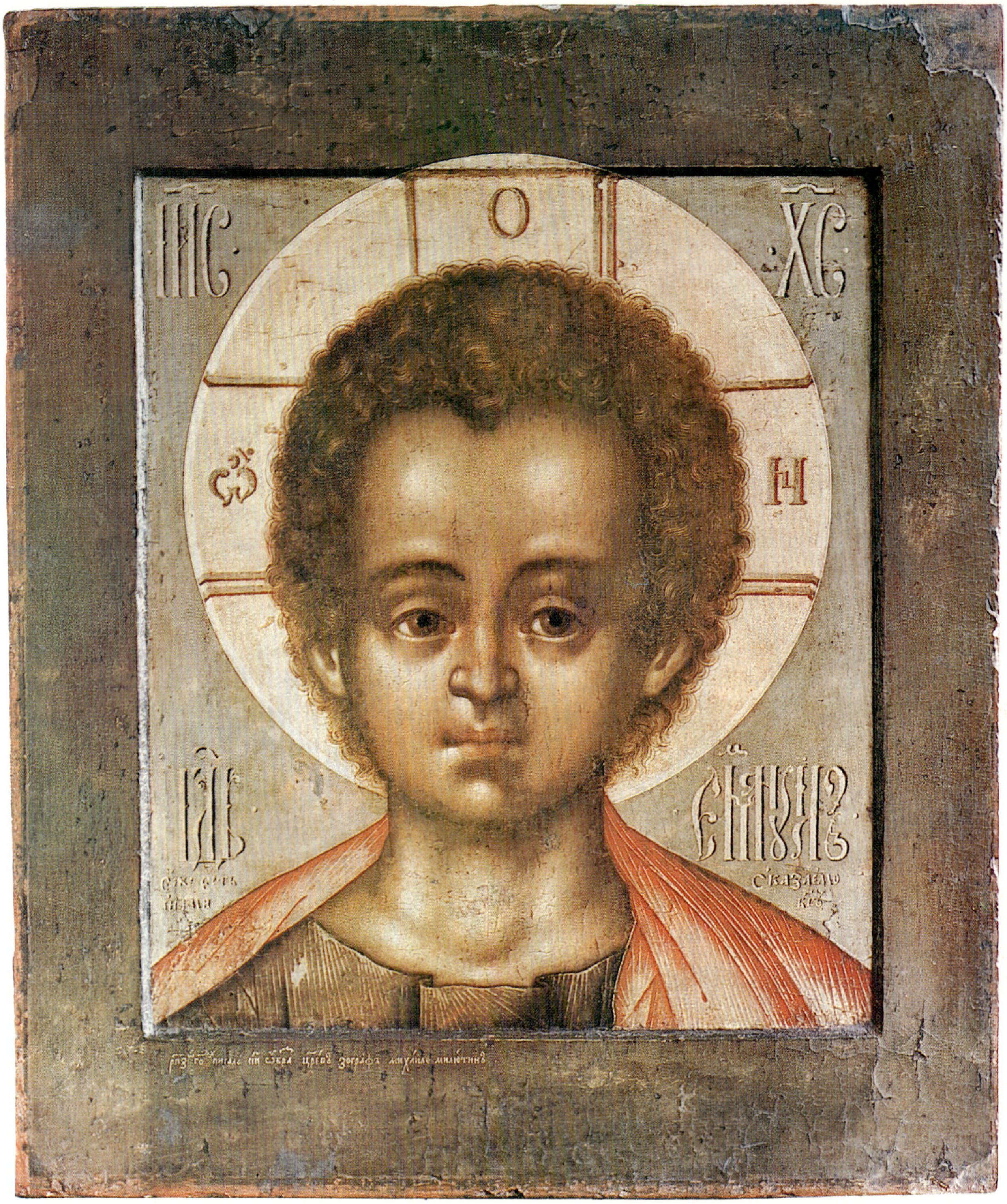

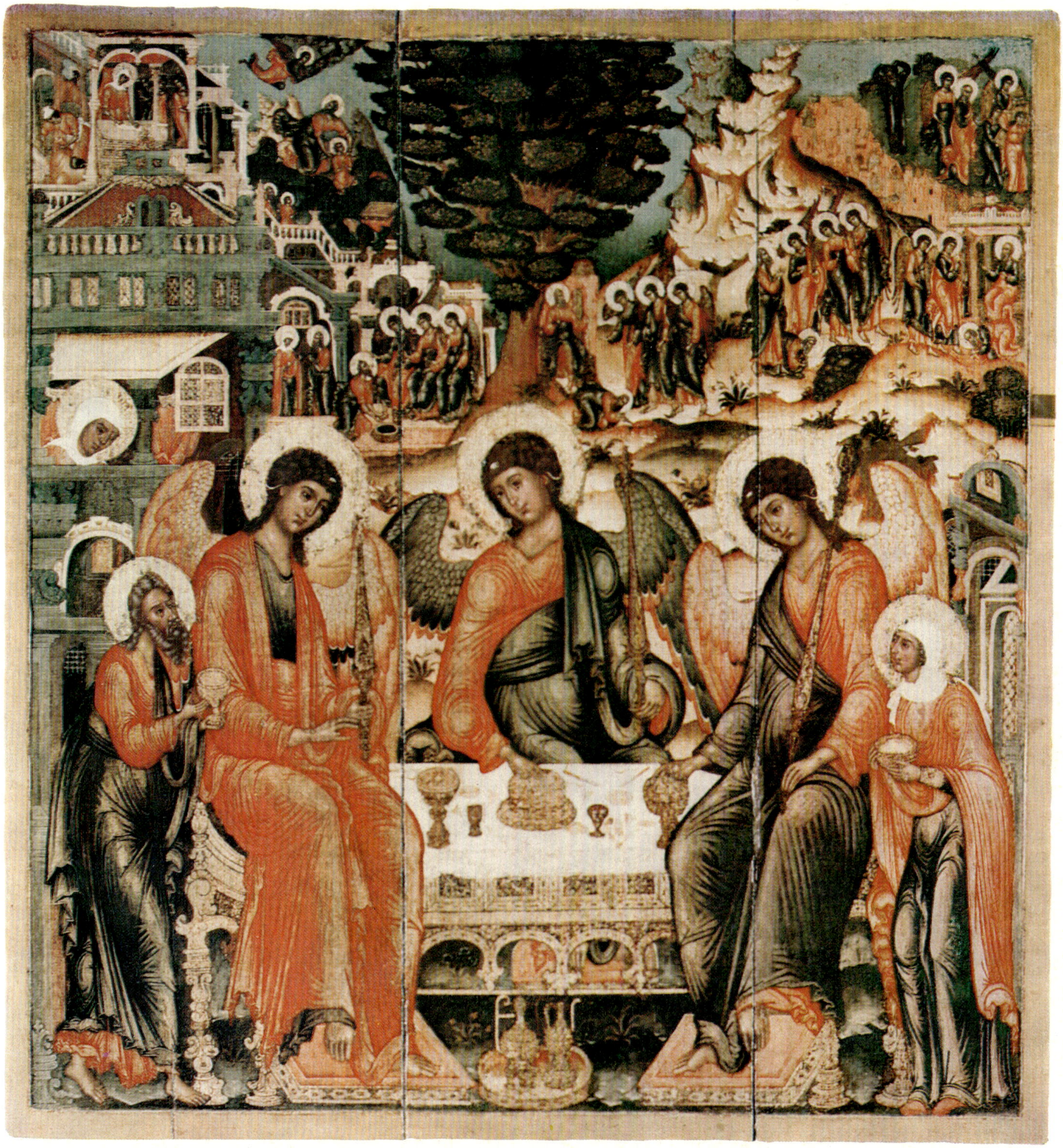

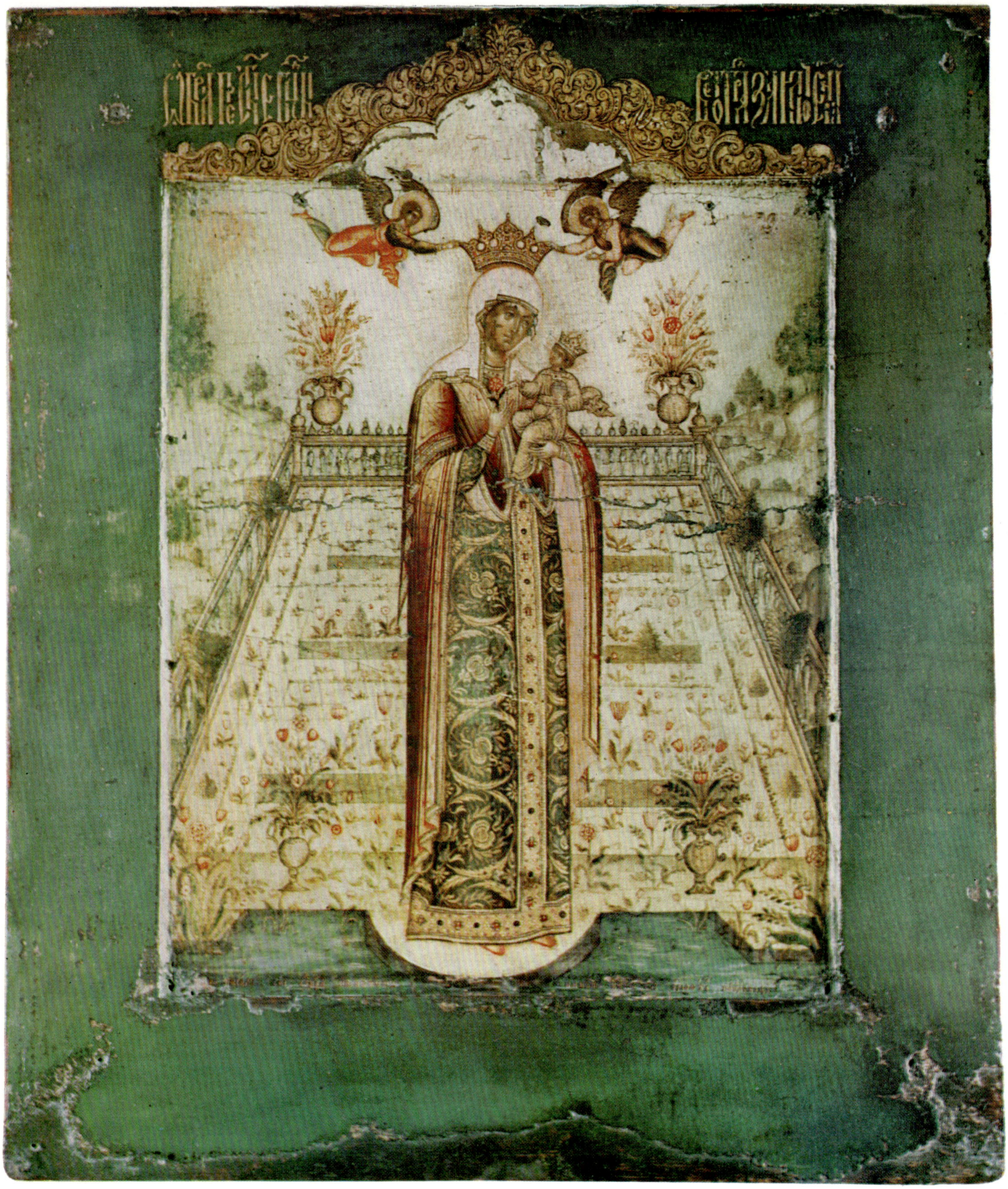

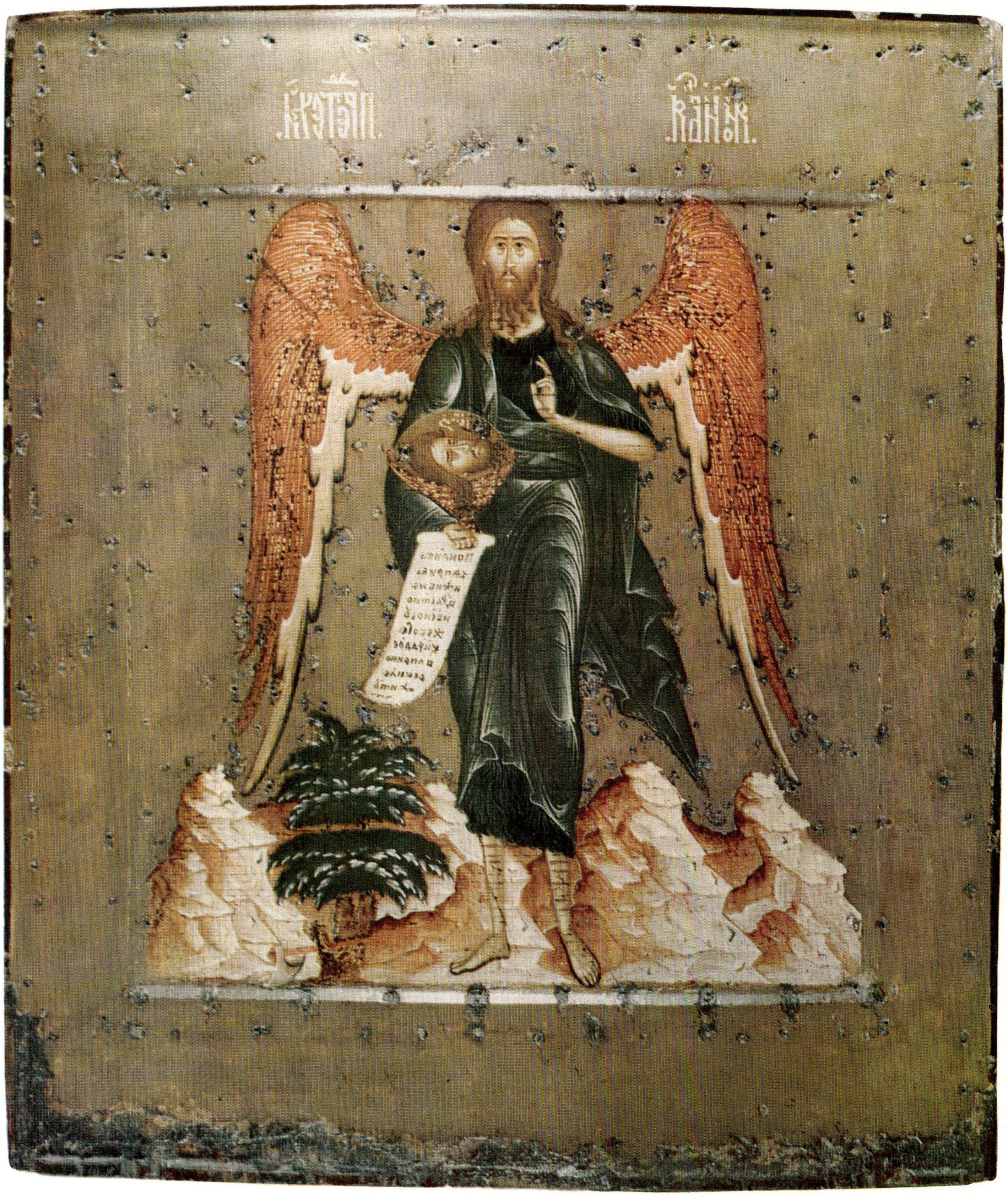

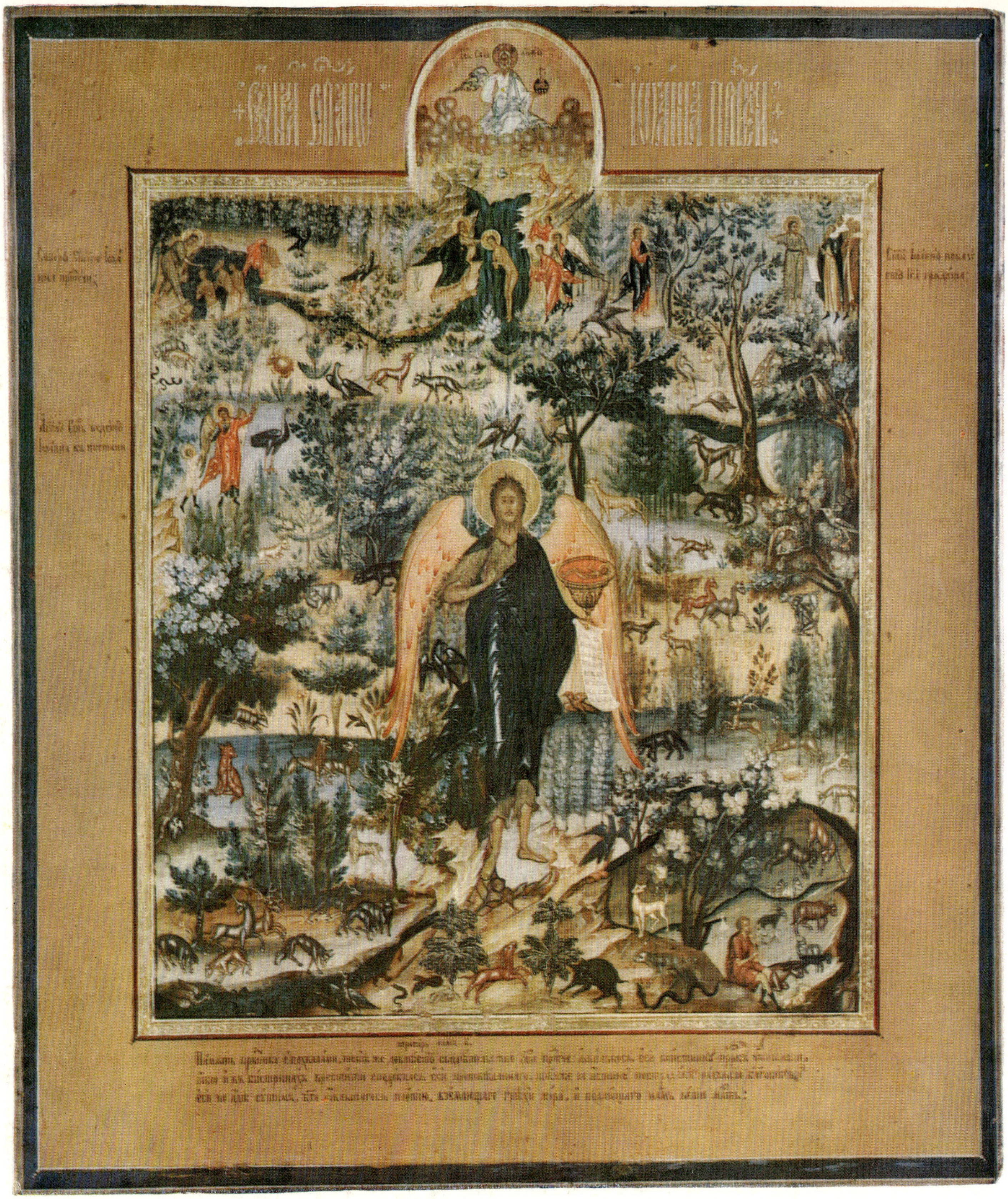